A Divine Alliance

How to Build Effective
Relationships Between
Apostles and Prophets

A DIVINE ALLIANCE

HOW TO BUILD EFFECTIVE RELATIONSHIPS BETWEEN APOSTLES AND PROPHETS

JIM LAFFOON

Wagner Publications

A Divine Alliance
Copyright © 2001
by Jim Laffoon
ISBN 1-58502-019-2

Published by
Wagner Publications
11005 N. Highway 83
Colorado Springs, CO 80921
www.wagnerpublications.org

Cover design by
Sage Design
6010 Grapevine Drive
80918
1-719-590-9164

Interior design by
Rebecca Sytsema

Rights for publishing this book in other languages are contracted by Gospel Literature International (GLINT). GLINT also provides technical help for the adaptation, translation, and publishing of Bible study resources and books in scores of languages worldwide. For further information, contact GLINT, P.O. Box 4060, Ontario, CA 91761-1003, USA. You may also send e-mail to glintint@aol.com, or visit their web site at www.glint.org.

1 2 3 4 5 6 7 8 9   07 06 05 04 03 02 01

CONTENTS

INTRODUCTION

I had the privilege of being born into an incredible Christian home. Although my parents had been taught to believe the miraculous gifts of the Holy Spirit had ceased at the end of the first century, their hunger for God led them into the baptism of the Holy Spirit in the 1960s. For the next fifteen years, they slowly transitioned their fundamentalist-type church into a vibrant, Spirit-filled congregation. They are still pastoring that church today.

As for apostles and prophets, however, our little church had only heard about those found on the pages of Scripture. Although my parents had ceased to question the possibility of their current existence, at that time there was no real understanding of the relevance or importance of these two governmental gifts. For me, however, this would soon change.

The Influence of Apostles and Prophets

When I reported to Fort Bragg, North Carolina, in 1972, I became part of a small, rapidly-growing church in Fayetteville. The pastor, Jerry Daley, had been influenced by a group of leaders who were part of the New Testament Church Movement, a tremendous revival that began in Waco, Texas, in 1946. Like the Latter Rain Movement, which began in 1948, this dynamic movement also involved the restoration of apostles and prophets to the church.

As Pastor Daley began to teach on the importance of apostles and prophets—and their relevance to our individual lives—I found myself wanting to really meet some of them. Men such as Tom Jones, Bobby Martz, Robert Ewing, and Ray Jennings began to come to our church. My life (as well as the lives of everyone in our church) was radically shaped by their preaching, prophecy, counsel, and example. Whether it was Bobby Martz prophesying the whole course of my ministry when I was only 22, or Jerry Daley (who was also an apostle) looking me in the eyes and telling me I was a prophet, apostles and prophets have shaped both my character and the course of my life for the past 28 years.

Today, aside from my relationship with Jesus (or with my wife and children), the greatest joy I experience comes from my relationships with the Apostolic Team of Morning Star International. Led by Rice Broocks, this incredible team of apostles and prophets is a continual source of counsel, care, and covering for my life. These are the spiritual leaders with whom God has called me to walk.

As you can obviously see, I believe in apostles and prophets. I not only believe in them, I receive from them as well. In fact, receiving from apostles and prophets is the very reason I wrote this book.

Walking With Apostles and Prophets

When I look at my last 26 years in the ministry, I have had the privilege of walking in relationships with apostles and prophets in many ways. I have walked with them as a local elder, a staff member, a senior pastor, and finally, as a member of an apostolic team. Therefore, whether you are reading this book as an apostle, prophet, senior pastor, local church leader, or faithful church member, I simply want to help you learn to receive the blessings that I have experienced.

Am I saying that all these relationships have always been free from pain and misunderstanding? No, obviously not. What I am saying is this: I would not be the man or the minister I am today without the impartation I have received from the apostles and prophets God has placed in my life. May God help all of us to better receive His gifts in this hour of worldwide restoration and visitation.

CHAPTER ONE

HOW APOSTLES AND PROPHETS OPERATE IN TODAY'S WORLD

W e live in an hour of unprecedented revival and harvest. As the Spirit of God moves across the face of the earth, churches are growing exponentially, and whole cities are being radically impacted by the gospel. Even in North America and Western Europe, the first embers of revival fire are already burning.

Yet, despite the magnitude of this incredible harvest, numbers alone will not build a strong church. In fact, I am convinced that we will not experience the full reality of Matthew 16:18 until we discover and deploy the gifted people through which Jesus has chosen to build His church: *And I tell you that you are Peter, and on this rock I will build my church, and the gates of Hades will not overcome it.*

These gifts to the church (gifted individuals) are discussed in Ephesians 4:7-16:

But to each one of us grace has been given as Christ ap-portioned it. This is why it says: "When he ascended on high, he led captives in his train and gave gifts to men." (What does 'he ascended' mean except that he also descended to the lower, earthly regions? He who descended is the very one who ascended higher than all the heavens, in order to fill the whole universe.) It was he who gave some to be apostles, some to be prophets, some to be evangelists, and some to be pastors and teachers, to prepare God's people for works of service, so that the body of Christ may be built up until we all reach unity in the faith and in the knowledge of the Son of God and become mature, attaining to the whole measure of the fullness of Christ. Then we will no longer be infants, tossed back and forth by the waves, and blown here and there by every wind of teaching and by the cunning and craftiness of men in their deceitful scheming. Instead, speaking the truth in love, we will in all things grow up into him who is the Head, that is, Christ. From him the whole body, joined and held together by every supporting ligament, grows and builds it-self up in love, as each part does its work.

Simply stated, when the ministry gifts of apostle, prophet, evangelist, teacher, and pastor are deployed in the church, the results are incredible. The church described in this passage is vibrant, mature, strong, and growing.

Although all these gift ministries are vital for building strong churches, in Ephesians 2:19-20 we find that two of these ministries in particular play a critical, foundation-laying role: *Consequently, you are no longer foreigners and aliens, but fellow citizens with God's people and members of God's house-hold, built on the foundation of the apostles and prophets, with Christ Jesus himself as the chief cornerstone.*

The strategic role played by these two ministries is also seen in the sequential priority they are given in 1 Corinthians

12:27-28: *"Now you are the body of Christ, and each one of you is a part of it. And in the church God has appointed first of all apostles, second prophets, third teachers, then workers of miracles, also those having gifts of healing, those able to help others, those with gifts of administration, and those speaking in different kinds of tongues."*

Let's take moment now to examine just a few aspects of the role of apostles and prophets in the church.

Apostles

After hundreds of years of being shrouded in unbelief and covered in dishonor, why is the restoration of the apostolic office so important to the church? After all, if we made it this far, why do we need it now?   There are many reasons why God has placed apostles first in the church (as we saw in 1 Corinthians 12:28). Let me share a few of them with you:

Apostles in Church Planting
As we see throughout the book of Acts, apostles are anointed church planters. Although each apostle can receive a different measure of the apostolic office, most of the ones I have met have received a grace from God to plant strong, healthy local churches. Whether they are planting the churches themselves or assisting others to do it, they have an anointing to bring a supernatural power and efficiency to this vital task.

If you have ever been part of a church plant that did not have an apostle leading it or at least assisting with it, you will need no convincing as to the importance of their ministry. I never cease to be amazed at the anointing God places on apostles to plant churches. Wherever they go, opportunities to plant churches seem to follow them. When an evangelist comes to a city, people are saved. When an apostle comes to the same city, people are saved—and a church is planted.

Apostles in Local Church Government

Apostles are involved in the government of the local church. Although every apostolic family of churches defines this aspect of the apostle's role differently, it is clear from the epistles written by Paul, John, and Peter that apostles have a vital role in the government of local churches. These are some of the governmental roles given to apostles in Scripture:

♦ **Apostles have the authority to intervene in church schisms and divisions:**

I appeal to you, brothers, in the name of our Lord Jesus Christ, that all of you agree with one another so that there may be no divisions among you and that you may be perfectly united in mind and thought. My brothers, some from Chloe's household have informed me that there are quarrels among you. What I mean is this: One of you says, "I follow Paul"; another, "I follow Apollos"; another, "I follow Cephas"; still another, "I follow Christ" (1 Cor 1:10-12).

Warn a divisive person once, and then warn him a second time. After that, have nothing to do with him. You may be sure that such a man is warped and sinful; he is self-condemned (Titus 3:10-11).

Imagine for a moment how much pain and destruction in the body of Christ could be avoided if every church, in times of internal division, had a trusted apostolic figure to turn to for counsel.

♦ **Apostles have the authority to deal with doctrinal heresy:**

I am astonished that you are so quickly deserting the

one who called you by the grace of Christ and are turning to a different gospel—which is really no gospel at all. Evidently some people are throwing you into confusion and are trying to pervert the gospel of Christ. But even if we or an angel from heaven should preach a gospel other than the one we preached to you, let him be eternally condemned! As we have already said, so now I say again: If anybody is preaching to you a gospel other than what you accepted, let him be eternally condemned! (Gal. 1:6-9).

♦ **Apostles have the authority to deal with immorality in local church leaders and in local churches:**

Do not entertain an accusation against an elder unless it is brought by two or three witnesses. Those who sin are to be rebuked publicly, so that the others may take warning (1 Tim. 5:19-20).

It is actually reported that there is sexual immorality among you, and of a kind that does not occur even among pagans: A man has his father's wife. And you are proud! Shouldn't you rather have been filled with grief and have put out of your fellowship the man who did this? Even though I am not physically present, I am with you in spirit. And I have already passed judgment on the one who did this, just as if I were present. When you are assembled in the name of our Lord Jesus and I am with you in spirit, and the power of our Lord Jesus is present, hand this man over to Satan, so that the sinful nature may be destroyed and his spirit saved on the day of the Lord (1 Cor. 5:1-5).

This aspect of the apostle's ministry is vital to the overall health of the church. Time after time, the body of Christ has been injured because biblical discipline has not been properly applied to the lives of leaders who have fallen into serious sin. Whether it is a public confession, the removal from ministry, or the wisdom and care needed to restore a fallen leader, God has equipped apostles for this task.

♦ **Apostles have the authority to set local church elders into office.**

It is clear from Scripture that apostles have a vital role to play in ordination of local church leadership. Acts 14:23 says, *Paul and Barnabas appointed elders for them in each church and, with prayer and fasting, committed them to the Lord, in whom they had put their trust.*

Titus 1:5 adds, *The reason I left you in Crete was that you might straighten out what was left unfinished and appoint elders in every town, as I directed you.*

Even in mature churches which have established local leadership teams, the role of apostles is critical in discerning character and calling. I cannot count the times pastors have had second thoughts about someone whom they had set into their local church leadership team. Maybe the ordination was premature, or they simply weren't truly gifted to do the job. Whatever the case may be, the process of discerning and developing leaders for a local church is one place where the wisdom of an apostle can be vital.

Apostles See Spiritual Destiny

Apostles are also gifted to recognize the calling and spiritual destiny in the lives of God's people. One of the most powerful examples of this aspect of the apostle's ministry is found in the book of Acts: *Joseph, a Levite from Cyprus, whom the apostles called Barnabas (which means Son of Encouragement), sold a field he owned and brought the money and put it at the apostles' feet* (Acts 4:36-37).

The word encouragement comes from the Greek word

nebee, which means prophet. Even as God renamed Abram, Jacob, and Simon according to their calling, the apostles in Jerusalem saw the prophetic calling on the life of Joseph, who was a businessman in the church, and redefined him accordingly. This is an amazing story. For the first time in history, God was allowing humans to rename people according to their spiritual destiny. That which had always been the prerogative of deity had now been given to humans through the apostolic office. It is no different today. God has given apostles the grace to perceive and define the calling and destiny of His people.

Apostles Move in the Miraculous

Many apostles are gifted to move in the miraculous. Whether it is the gift of faith or the gift of miracles, they have the ability to bring the supernatural power of God to bear in the lives of nations, churches, cities, and people. The lives of the apostles with whom I walk are filled with examples of God's miraculous provision and power, especially as they plant churches and advance the kingdom of God around the world. In fact, church planting and evangelism are the very purpose for which this miraculous power has been given to apostles:

He called his twelve disciples to him and gave them authority to drive out evil spirits and to heal every disease and sickness...As you go, preach this message: "The kingdom of heaven is near." Heal the sick, raise the dead, cleanse those who have leprosy, drive out demons. Freely you have received, freely give (Matt. 10:1,7-8).

I will not venture to speak of anything except what Christ has accomplished through me in leading the Gentiles to obey God by what I have said and done—by the power of signs and miracles, through the power of the Spirit. So from Jerusalem all the way around to Illyricum, I have fully proclaimed the gospel of Christ. It has always been my ambition to preach the gospel where Christ was not known, so that I would not be building on someone else's foundation (Rom. 15:18-20).

An example of this miraculous anointing can be seen in the life of one of the apostles with whom I walk. Greg Ball has been uniquely gifted by God to reach the sports world. As different professional sports team members respond to the gospel, we plant churches in the cities where these sports teams are located. During the 1997 National Football League season, Mark Brunell, the quarterback of the Jacksonville Jaguars, injured his knee. After a thorough examination of his knee, the doctors concluded that he had ligament tear, which is normally a season-ending injury.

After the diagnosis, Greg flew into Jacksonville and prayed for Mark. The doctors had decided to scope his knee and repair it immediately. They were sure that their diagnosis would be confirmed when the knee was scoped. Mark, however, believed his knee had been healed when Greg prayed for him. He boldly told his doctors he had received a miracle. When the doctors saw Mark's divinely-repaired knee, they were stunned. Mark, who was awake during the procedure, said, "One doctor simply pointed at me, then pointed toward heaven." The other doctor said, "I want to go to his church!" This is just one of the many examples I could give of the operation of the gifts of healing or miracles through the life of an apostle.

Apostles Deploy God's People

The very word apostle means sent one. As sent ones (those who burn for the mission of God), they have the unique ability to help individuals (and even churches) discover and fulfill the reason why they were sent to this planet. As we will see in the next two passages, however, their gifting goes far beyond merely helping people to recognize their callings. Apostles have been given authority by God to deploy His people into the harvest through what we will call apostolic sending:

When the apostles in Jerusalem heard that Samaria had accepted the word of God, they sent Peter and John to them. When they arrived, they prayed for them that they might receive the Holy Spirit, because the Holy Spirit had not yet come upon any of them; they had simply been baptized into the name of the Lord Jesus. Then Peter and John placed their hands on them, and they received the Holy Spirit (Acts 8:14-17).

News of this reached the ears of the church at Jerusalem, and they sent Barnabas to Antioch. When he arrived and saw the evidence of the grace of God, he was glad and encouraged them all to remain true to the Lord with all their hearts. He was a good man, full of the Holy Spirit and faith, and a great number of people were brought to the Lord (Acts 11:22-24).

I am convinced that apostolic sending will play a vital role in the fulfillment of the Great Commission. Most Christians do not know that in the New Testament, the Lord had two ways of deploying His people into the harvest. The first of these ways was being led by the Holy Spirit. The second method was being sent by the Holy Spirit through an apostle.

Although the Holy Spirit is involved in both methods, the sequence is different. When you are being directly led by the Holy Spirit, your deployment is initiated by the Holy Spirit. It is then confirmed by the leaders God has placed in your life. On the other hand, when you are being sent by an apostle, your deployment is through a human vessel (the apostle), and it should be confirmed by the Holy Spirit in your heart. Although both of these methods are obliviously valid, I believe more and more people will be deployed through apostolic sending as the office of the apostle is restored to the church.

In fact, this may be the most critical role played by apostles in this hour. I am convinced when apostles are given their rightful place in a local church, the people in that church will come to a whole new place of finding and fulfilling the very purposes for which they were born.

If this is to happen, however, we must accept the fact that apostles, not just prophets, have been given authority by God to speak direction and destiny into the lives of God's people. Although they may not use phrases like, "Thus saith the Lord," or, "The Lord would say unto thee," apostles have been gifted by God to deploy His people into the harvest.

Apostle John Eckhardt, from Chicago, likens this aspect of apostolic ministry to the story of the blind man who was healed after washing in the Pool of Siloam (John 9:1-7): *As he went along, he saw a man blind from birth. His disciples asked him, "Rabbi, who sinned, this man or his parents, that he was born blind?"*

'Neither this man nor his parents sinned," said Jesus, "but this happened so that the work of God might be displayed in his life. As long as it is day, we must do the work of him who sent me. Night is coming, when no one can work. While I am in the world, I am the light of the world." Having said this, he spit on the ground, made some mud with the saliva, and put it on the man's eyes. "Go," he told him, "wash in the Pool of Siloam" (this word means Sent). So the man went and washed, and came home seeing.

According to John, many Christians are just like the blind man in this story. Although Jesus has touched them, they are still blind – blind to their purpose and destiny. When they wash in the pool of Siloam (sent), however, they will see the apostolic purpose of God for their lives.

Like John Eckhardt, I believe until a Christian washes in the pool of apostolic ministry, he or she will remain partially blind to the very reasons for which he or she was born. Furthermore, I am convinced that thousands of Christians are sitting beside the roadway of destiny, waiting for someone to bring them to the pool of Siloam – the place of apostolic destiny.

Prophets

Although prophets such as Bill Hamon have written a number of excellent books on prophetic ministry, I still want to take a moment to describe their practical role in the body of Christ. Before I describe their specific roles, however, it is important to remember that prophets are not simply anointed people who give personal prophecies to individuals. True mature prophets, depending on the measure of the gift they have received, have the supernatural ability to perceive and proclaim the immediate word of the Lord to individuals, churches, cities, and nations. They are anointed by God to discern demonic attacks, to reveal divine strategies, to recognize callings and giftings, and to impart prophetic gifts. They also accurately proclaim, through preaching or prophecy, what God is saying at that moment to specific churches and individuals. More specifically, these are some of the critical roles prophets have been called to fulfill in the church.

Prophets See Into the Invisible World

Prophets have the ability to look into the invisible world, perceiving both the operation of the demonic and the angelic in people and places (1 Kings 22:16-24; 2 Kings 2:9-10; 2 Kings 8:23). The practical application of this anointing can be seen in spiritual mapping, demon deliverance, and other forms of spiritual warfare. I have repeatedly seen prophets—using gifts of discernment—reveal demonic bondage in the lives of individuals as well as churches.

The importance of this aspect of prophetic ministry can be seen in a recent example. My home church purchased a building to house our various ministries. For the three years leading up to the time of this writing, we have fought to obtain a "conditional use" permit. The legal implications of our battle have been so strategic, it has made the national news. Finally, even as I am writing, we are winning! Behind this incredible victory have been apostolic authority, prophetic discernment, and concerted worldwide prayer. Whether it was the very name of the witch who was leading ground-level spiritual warfare against us, or the discernment of which principalities we were facing, prophetic ministry has played a key role in our struggle. Without it, we would not have won.

Prophets See God's Giftings in His People

Prophets recognize the callings and giftings of God in the lives of His people. Even as Samuel recognized the call of God on David, an obscure, rejected shepherd boy, so prophets today are used by God to confirm these callings.

I'll never forget my first life-changing prophecy. I was twenty-one, going to Bible College, and working part-time on the church staff. A prophet named Bobby Martz called me out of the audience and gave me a detailed prophecy about ministering to the nations of the world. I can still describe the power and awe I felt as that humble man of God defined the very reason for which I was born. It gave me the confidence I needed to pursue God's destiny for my life. Today, twenty-three years later, I am walking in the fulfillment of that word. I have seen this type of prophetic confirmation repeated in the lives of God's people over and over again around the world.

Prophets Can Affect the Spiritual Climate of a Local Church

Third, prophets bring the supernatural reality of prophecy to local churches. When a mature, accurate gift of prophecy is expressed in the local church, the church will be strengthened both corporately and individually (see Acts 15:32; 1 Cor. 14:3). As both a pastor and a prophet, I have found a prophetic service can bring more encouragement to a local church than almost any other single thing. Whether you have one prophet (or a team of prophets), people are so hungry to hear from the Lord that they will come out—no matter when you have the meeting! Whenever we would have a prophetic service in the church I pastored; the spiritual climate of the church would be dramatically altered for weeks. Even those who did not receive prophecies would be touched as they saw the lives of their friends opened up through the gift of prophecy.

Prophets Bring Power Evangelism to the Church

As our society becomes more and more postmodern, this aspect of the prophetic ministry will become critical. I say this because one aspect of the rise of postmodernism in our culture has been a return to premodern forms of spirituality. Many people readily accept the reality of an invisible realm, filled with spiritual forces and beings.

In this climate, gifts like prophecy and the word of knowledge can be very effective tools of evangelism. An example of the evangelistic power of these gifts can be seen in the story of the woman at the well in John 4:

"I have no husband," she replied. Jesus said to her, "You are right when you say you have no husband. The fact is, you

have had five husbands, and the man you now have is not your husband. What you have just said is quite true."

Many of the Samaritans from that town believed in him because of the woman's testimony, "He told me everything I ever did." (John 4:17-18, 39)

Just like the woman at the well, I have seen scores of unsaved people touched through the operation of prophecy and the word of knowledge. Over and over again, I have watched these precious souls weep under the anointing of God—as the secrets of their hearts were revealed through prophecy. This should not surprise us, because it is a direct fulfillment of 1 Corinthians 14:23-25:

So if the whole church comes together and everyone speaks in tongues, and some who do not understand or some unbelievers come in, will they not say that you are out of your mind? But if an unbeliever or someone who does not understand comes in while everybody is prophesying, he will be convinced by all that he is a sinner and will be judged by all, and the secrets of his heart will be laid bare. So he will fall down and worship God, exclaiming, "God is really among you!"

Although prophetic evangelism is still almost never practiced in the body of Christ, I am convinced that we are coming to an hour where the realities this passage describes will become normal. I already know of churches and ministries who are setting aside whole services for prophetic evangelism. The results have already been staggering. In one such service, a whole family was shaken and two of the sons were saved when the Lord revealed through a word of knowledge that they had been robbed at gunpoint. This is only one example out of the many I could give which illustrate the power of prophetic evangelism.

Prophets Bring Direction, Correction, and Confirmation

Through prophetic preaching and prophesying, mature prophets bring timely prophetic direction, correction, and confirmation to local churches. Although personal prophecy is tremendous, prophetic preaching is also vital. In fact, when I was pastoring, I considered a timely prophetic message more important than a long string of personal prophecies. Over and over again, the Lord confirmed our church's direction (down to the very words I had been using to describe it) through a message from a visiting prophet. Whether the prophetic message was delivered through a prophecy or a sermon, God used it mightily.

Prophets Are Watchmen

As watchmen, prophets are called to protect the church and its leaders. This aspect of prophetic ministry is beautifully reflected in Hosea 9:8: *The prophet, along with my God, is the watchman over Ephraim...*

When the Bible says "watchman," it does not mean "watchdog." Prophets are not simply called to snarl and growl at the church. They are called to lovingly watch over the people of God and to keep them from harm. Although there are times they must bring warnings to individuals, churches, and/or nations, even then their motivation should be one of loving protection. In the ministry God has given me, one of my greatest joys is to protect the men with whom I have been called to walk. Over and over again, God has used me to protect them and their families from harm. Whether it has been bad water on the mission field, or breathing problems in the middle of the night, God has revealed things like this to me by the word of knowledge. I am convinced that this is one of the most important aspects of prophetic ministry.

Prophets Bring Judgment and Interpretation

Prophets are also used to bring judgment and interpretation to prophecies, dreams, and visions. Whether it was Daniel interpreting the king's dreams, or Paul's charge to prophets to judge prophecy (1 Corinthians 14:29), this is a vital part of prophetic ministry. I have seen individuals (and even whole churches) thrown off course by a prophecy that was not judged or a misinterpreted dream or vision. Whether it is the misguided ravings of a person who is simply immature in the use of their gift, or the curses of a real false prophet, this is the time where the clarity and judgment of a mature prophet is needed.

The Real Battle

When you consider the vital God-given role of apostles and prophets, it is no wonder that the enemy has steadfastly resisted their restoration to the church. At times, anti-supernaturalism and rationalism have blinded the church to the reality of apostles and prophets in the present day. In other cases, tremendous pain has been felt because of the immaturity and misunderstandings which have sometimes accompanied the restoration of these roles. Whichever the case may be, the road to recovering the fullness of these incredible gifts has been fraught with peril.

I am convinced that our battle has never been with the Christians who have disputed the present reality of these ministry gifts. No. All the discourse and argumentation have simply hidden the real enemy from our eyes. Satan himself fears the restoration of these gifts. He fears them because he knows that the gates of hell will never prevail against a church built on the foundation of apostles and prophets.

CHAPTER TWO

THE RELATIONSHIP BETWEEN APOSTLES AND PROPHETS

As anointed as apostles and prophets are individually in building the church, their effectiveness rises exponentially when they are deployed as a team. Whether it was Jesus and John the Baptist or Paul and Silas, this dynamic ministry combination played a critical role in both founding and building the church of the New Testament. In this present age, if we are to build strong, lasting, world-changing churches, we must rediscover the secrets of apostolic and prophetic teamwork.

This, then, is the subject of this chapter. How can apostles and prophets effectively work together? In order to be as clear as possible, we will discuss this critical subject by examining the problems faced by apostles and prophets who attempt to work together. Then we will consider several pictures of apostolic/prophetic teams in the New Testament. Finally, we

will discuss the principles needed for apostles and prophets to
work together effectively.

The Problems

A Perilous Relationship

First, when one looks at the body of Christ today, true apos-
tolic/prophetic teamwork is almost nonexistent. Whether it
was prophetic words that never came to pass, harsh delivery
styles, or revelations so esoteric they were of no practical value,
many apostles and other governmental leaders have had bad
experiences with prophets. These experiences are also compounded by the fact that many prophets, on a functional level,
reject all human authority in spiritual matters. Simply stated,
if they believe God has spoken to them, no human can tell
them differently. As a prophet myself, I know well the temptation toward a radical form of mysticism which can make a
person's spiritual senses the final authority in his life.

On the other hand, many prophets have been badly
wounded by well-meaning apostles and pastors. I cannot count
the prophetic individuals who have been crushed (under the
guise of biblical correction) by a leader who was either threatened by the nature of their giftings or frustrated by their lack
of maturity.

Why has a relationship with such divine potential been so
perilous? First it is because, like all human relationships, sins
such as pride, insecurity, jealousy, ambition, and rebellion have
impaired the relationships of these gifted individuals. Without the realities of biblical forgiveness, humility, and
submission to authority, apostles and prophets will never be
able to relate together, no matter how many books are written
or sermons are preached on the subject.

Old Testament Model of the Prophet

Second, many prophets have modeled their ministries after the Old Testament model of the prophet. I do not know whether they have adopted this model because the Old Testament model of the prophet is more appealing to their ego, or simply because the role of the prophet is more clearly delineated in the Old Testament. Whatever the case may be, I have observed two things: First, many prophets relate to the church like Old Testament prophets related to Israel. Second, many prophets relate to apostles and pastors as their Old Testament counterparts related to their leaders—kings. For the purpose of this study, however, we will concentrate on the second of these two observations.

In the Old Testament, prophets functioned independently of both the kings and the priesthood. Except in cases where they were being mentored by an older prophet, they were accountable only to God. Although they would treat the godly kings with respect and deference, prophets' relationship with the kings basically involved four aspects:

◆ First, the prophets were used to anoint the kings. Although they did not normally officially crown the kings, their act of anointing them with oil was a critical step in the process of coronation. An example of this can be seen in Samuel's anointing of David (1 Sam. 16:1-13).

◆ Second, the Old Testament prophets were the conscience of the nations as well as of the kings who led them. This aspect of their ministry can be seen in the life of Jeremiah, who served as Judah's national conscience for years, even though both the citizens and the kings refused to accept the possibility of God judging them through the Babylonians.

◆ Third, sometimes the prophets confronted the kings. Whether it was Elijah's confrontation with Ahab (1 Kings 18:1-19) or Samuel rebuking Saul (1 Samuel 15:12-31), the prophets of the Old Testament were faithful to confront the kings of Israel and Judah.

◆ Fourth, the prophets brought tremendous consolation to the kings. Even the apostate King Ahab received prophetic encouragement and comfort before the most strategic battle of his life (1 Kings 20:13-30).

Obviously, many of these aspects of the prophet's ministry are still valid today. There are times when a prophet must confront an apostle or a pastor. Furthermore, God does use prophets to discern and reveal apostolic callings in the lives of leaders. Even serving as a conscience for a nation, church, or leader has its place in this hour. As for prophetic consolation and encouragement, it is always needed. Yet, as a stand-alone model, the Old Testament understanding of a prophet is at best incomplete—and at its worst, extremely dangerous.

In order to understand the problems inherent with the Old Testament model, we must take a few minutes to examine the relationship between apostles and prophets in the New Testament. In order to facilitate this examination, we will study the four pairs of relationships: Jesus and John the Baptist; Paul and Barnabas; Paul and Silas; and Paul and Agabus.

Biblical Pictures of Apostolic/Prophetic Relationship

Jesus and John the Baptist
In the relationship of Jesus and John the Baptist, we find a powerful example of an apostolic/prophetic team. Although

all the gifts and ministry were operational in Jesus, He is obviously the apostolic founder of Christianity (Heb. 3:1). As for John, we find in Luke 7:26-27 that he was one of history's most important prophets. John 1:32-37 reveals two critical aspects of their relationship:

Then John gave this testimony: "I saw the Spirit come down from heaven as a dove and remain on him. I would not have known him, except that the one who sent me to baptize with water told me, 'The man on whom you see the Spirit come down and remain is he who will baptize with the Holy Spirit.' I have seen and I testify that this is the Son of God."

The next day John was there again with two of his disciples. When he saw Jesus passing by, he said, "Look, the Lamb of God!" When the two disciples heard him say this, they followed Jesus.

Here we find that John was used to recognize Jesus. Through his prophetic relationship with the Lord, he was able to look beyond the fact that Jesus was his younger cousin and could discern the hand of the Father on His life. Fortunately, John's ministry did not stop at simply recognizing the apostolic anointing. In this passage we also find that John was also called to reveal the true identity and anointing of Jesus. This was the primary purpose of John's life. He was called to say to the crowds, "This is the man you need to follow."

As a prophet, I have found both of these roles are critical in this present hour. In the family of churches of which I am a part (Morning Star International), I have been used repeatedly in both conferences and churches to reveal apostles and their strategic importance to the churches and people whom they serve. I am convinced that even as John prepared the way for Jesus, so prophets today are called to prepare the way for a new generation of apostles to do their work.

Let me illustrate what I mean by preparing the way.

Through the power of the prophetic office, prophets can forge the credibility necessary to speak to the most sensitive areas in the lives of churches and people. For example, many times churches bring me in to speak because they love the supernatural gift of prophecy. What they really need, however, is some practical apostolic wisdom to solve the complex problems they are facing. When I find myself in situations like this, I use my prophetic credibility to point them to the apostolic help they need.

In the relationship between Jesus and John the Baptist, we also find one of the great tests of prophetic ministry. This test is described in two passages in John:

Now this was John's testimony when the Jews of Jerusalem sent priests and Levites to ask him who he was. He did not fail to confess, but confessed freely, "I am not the Christ." (John 1:19-20)

They came to John and said to him, "Rabbi, that man who was with you on the other side of the Jordan—the one you testified about—well, he is baptizing, and everyone is going to him." To this John replied, "A man can receive only what is given him from heaven. You yourselves can testify that I said, 'I am not the Christ but am sent ahead of him.' The bride belongs to the bridegroom. The friend who attends the bridegroom waits and listens for him, and is full of joy when he hears the bridegroom's voice. That joy is mine, and it is now complete. He must become greater; I must become less." (John 3:26-30).

"Who are you, John?" This question precipitated the defining moment of John's life. After all, no greater prophet had ever been born than John. The crowds, drawn by the anointing on his life, were the greatest seen in Israel for centuries. They were even coming into the desert to hear his clarion call to repentance and holiness. Surely, like Elijah, he was the physical embodiment of everything God was doing on the earth. He had been the one who would apostolically plant the kingdom of God on the earth! Yet, he was not the One, and he knew it. With these words he passed his test: "I am not the Christ, but am sent ahead of Him."

This test is still going on today. Although they may not realize it, many prophets are facing the same test that John faced. The anointing of God on their lives is drawing crowds. Everyone wants a personal prophecy or revelation from these people. Whole conferences want to bask in the prophetic phenomenon that surrounds their lives. Even churches are clamoring to come under their prophetic covering.

If prophets choose to become a covering independent of all true apostolic government, they are either self-proclaimed (or proclaimed so by well-meaning friends) to be an apostle or prophetic-apostle. Although the churches in the network they establish will benefit from the prophetic anointing, they will lack the church planting and governing, nation-opening, pioneering power that results from apostolic leadership.

I personally know this test well. There was a time in my life when I was ready to proclaim I was an apostle. Churches wanted my help, pastors asked for my covering, and everyone wanted a prophecy. This brief period was the only time in my ministry that I had ever been independent of apostolic authority. Now I am so thankful that God spared me from a life of trying to be something He had never called me to be. He united me with a tremendous team of apostles who are committed to planting churches throughout the world.

Paul and Barnabas

The next apostolic/prophetic relationship we will discuss is the one between Paul and Barnabas. Although it is obvious that Paul is an apostle, many Christian leaders would contend that Barnabas is also an apostle. Their contention is based on the facts that Barnabas was sent out on an apostolic mission with Paul from the church in Antioch (Acts 13:1-3), and that he, along with Paul, is referred to as an apostle (Acts 14:4). Although they may well be right, my opinion is that the primary gift in the life of the Barnabas was either a prophet or what C. Peter Wagner would call a hyphenated apostle (a prophet-apostle). Whatever the case may be, I believe the office of the prophet was the strongest anointing in the life of Barnabas.

My first reason for this opinion is that the apostles changed his name from Joseph to Barnabas (Acts 4:36). The name Barnabas comes from a Chaldean word which means "son of prophecy." I believe his name change was a reflection of the call and anointing the apostles saw on his life. My other reason is that Barnabas was far senior to Paul in the ministry when their relationship began. He was the very man God used to both recognize the apostolic anointing on the life of Paul and to reveal it to the church of that day (Acts 9:26-30 and 11:25-26). Yet, by the time they left Cyprus, one of the stops on their first apostolic journey, Paul was already in charge of the team.

This leadership transition is reflected in the language of Acts 13. In verse 2, the Holy Spirit said, *"Set apart for me Barnabas and Saul for the work to which I have called them."* By the time we get to verse 13, their team is referred to as *"Paul and his companions."* Was this clear change in leadership a demotion for Barnabas because of some problem in his life? No. It simply illustrated the fact that apostles have been given more governmental authority than prophets (1 Cor. 12:28).

As a prophet, I both recognize and enjoy the fact that God has put my life under apostolic authority. When I think of

Rice Broocks, Phil Bonasso, and Steve Murrell (the three apostolic men God used to establish the ministry of which I am a part), my heart is filled with thankfulness for their leadership. As the senior prophetic leader in our ministry, I am given all the influence, authority, and opportunities I could ever desire.

Yet, I even have something more than that. I have had the fulfillment of seeing the anointing and fruitfulness of the ministry God has given me increase exponentially because I am ministering in divine concert with apostolically gifted men. In a ministry filled with apostles and evangelists, I don't just prophesy about the coming harvest; I live in the middle of it! Furthermore, I do more than prophesy about church planting and pray that it will happen. I have the privilege of ministering in church plants around the world because I have chosen to walk with the men gifted by God to do the work of planting churches. Whether it is Barnabas or myself, we cannot forget that all prophets must settle the question of who is in authority.

Paul and Silas

After his separation from Barnabas, Paul invited Silas to join his ministry team (Acts 15:40). We know from Acts 15:32 that Silas was a prophet. Once again, Paul had been divinely teamed with the prophetic. The rest is history; God used Paul and Silas to open up the whole province of Macedonia.

It is also interesting to note what happened in the province of Macedonia when Silas was not with Paul. Although it is only speculation, I have wondered if one of the reasons for the meager fruit produced by Paul's ministry in the city of Athens (Acts 17:32-34) was the fact that Silas was not with him (Acts 17:14). Was Paul missing the supernatural revelation and insight into the invisible realm which Silas could have provided?

As I have already said, all we can really do is speculate.

Although Scripture is virtually silent on the subject on workings of apostolic/prophetic teamwork, I have learned from my own experience that the ministry productivity of apostles and prophets increases exponentially when they are teamed together. One of the reasons I believe this is because when the revelation of a prophet is combined with the wisdom of an apostle, there is a whole new level of strategic application.

In my own life, I have seen the apostles with whom I work receive the wisdom of God to apply the revelation I receive from Him—and our working together brings incredible results. Another reason is because the insights prophets receive into God's strategy and timing for nations, cities, and people are an incredible help to an apostolic church planter. Last, the combination of prophetic anointing, along with the signs and wonders that can accompany apostolic ministry, creates an incredible atmosphere for Kingdom advancement. I am convinced that this potent ministry combination will be one of the keys to completing the Great Commission.

Paul and Agabus

The last apostolic/prophetic relationship we will discuss is the one between Paul and Agabus. Although they were not in an intimate team relationship, God used this respected prophet (Acts 11:27-30), to speak into Paul's life at a critical time in his ministry:

After we had been there a number of days, a prophet named Agabus came down from Judea. Coming over to us, he took Paul's belt, tied his own hands and feet with it and said, "The Holy Spirit says, 'In this way the Jews of Jerusalem will bind the owner of this belt and will hand him over to the Gentiles.'" When we heard this, we and the people there pleaded with Paul not to go up to Jerusalem. Then Paul answered, "Why are you weeping and breaking my heart? I am ready not only to be bound, but also to die in Jerusalem for the name of the Lord Jesus" (Acts 21:10-13).

From this unique prophetic encounter, we can extract two observations. First, it is critical that apostles be open to receiving prophetic ministry from proven prophets, even ones who are not in a team relationship with them. At times, a prophet who is not intimately acquainted with a person's life can speak even more accurately, because the word is not affected by their natural knowledge.

In addition, through the prophetic gift, prophets can bring to apostles some revelation vital to their ministry. Whether it is a warning, encouragement, or comfort, this aspect of the prophet's ministry cannot be minimized. I never cease to be amazed by the power of God to encourage even the most seasoned apostle through a simple word of prophecy.

Guiding Principles of Apostolic/Prophetic Relationships

As we come to the end of this chapter, let me take moment to lay out what I consider to be some of the guiding principles of relationships between apostles and prophets.

Principle 1: Although there is much to be learned from the Old Testament model of prophets (prophets as independent ministers who are accountable to no one but God), it is not the pattern of New Testament church life.

Principle 2: God has placed the office of the apostle over the office of the prophet (1 Cor. 12:28). Simply stated, prophets function most effectively when they are under the covering of apostles.

Principle 3: One of the hardest of all relationships to successfully negotiate are those between peers. Even though God
has placed apostles in authority over prophets, many times
they will also be peers and even intimate friends. When
this is the case, mutual respect, humility, and submission
to one to another are even more critical. Even though the
ministry team I am a part of is led by apostles, we all hold
each other accountable, in love, for our marriages, families, lives, and ministries.

Principle 4: Although God has placed apostles over prophets, prophets have an unique ability to bring strength,
encouragement, revelation, and comfort to apostles. Therefore, it is vital that apostles be open to the ministry of the
prophet.

Principle 5: The fruitfulness of apostles and prophets can
increase exponentially when they are willing to work as a
team. Whether it is the revelation provided by the prophet,
or the wisdom and governmental grace of the apostle, these
ministries have an ability to complement one another. This
is an unique relationship in the kingdom of God.

Before I close this chapter, let me say that although the
information contained here can be very helpful when it is applied, no relationship between an apostle and a prophet, or
even one between a pastor and a person with the gift of prophecy, can experience long-term success without the biblical
attitudes described in 1 Corinthians 13:4-8:

*Love is patient, love is kind. It does not envy, it does not
boast, it is not proud. It is not rude, it is not self-seeking, it is*

not easily angered, it keeps no record of wrongs. Love does not delight in evil but rejoices with the truth. It always protects, always trusts, always hopes, always perseveres. Love never fails.

It does not matter if you are the most seasoned apostle or prophet, or the newest leader in your church. If you do not have patience, kindness, forgiveness, the ability to trust, and a lifestyle of humility, long-term ministry teamwork (and deep relationships in general) will be almost impossible for you to maintain. May God build all of these vital characteristics into our lives as we seek to birth apostolic/prophetic teams that will shake, in our generation, all the nations of the world!

CHAPTER THREE

THE RELATIONSHIP
AMONG PROPHETS

We live in an hour when prophets and prophecy are rapidly gaining acceptance throughout the body of Christ. Untold thousands, and maybe even millions, of believers, and the churches they represent, have been strengthened through the operation of these amazing gifts. Although the specific protocol and practical operation of prophets and prophecy will probably be debated until Christ returns, their value (and validity) among the estimated 500 million Pentecostals and charismatics in our world is virtually unchallenged.

Even more interesting is the fact that the return to premodern forms of spirituality, which have accompanied the rise of postmodernism in the Western world, has also created a new openness to the supernatural within our culture. Long relegated to societal fringe groups, extrasensory phenomena like visions, dreams, prophecy, and spiritual beings are now entering the mainstream of popular consciousness and thought.

Yet, if the church is to capture this strategic moment, prophets must come to a whole new level of maturity, accuracy, and power. For this to happen, I am convinced that we must discover new models of prophetic ministry. Part of this remodeling process involves the whole concept of how prophets relate to one another. Although much could be said about prophetic relationships, in the scope of this chapter we will only discuss two types of relationships: mentoring and ministry. In section one, we will discuss prophetic mentoring in the lives of Samuel and the school of the prophets: Elijah and Elisha, and Elisha and Gehazi. In section two, we will examine prophetic ministry teams from the lives of Judas and Silas as well as the two witnesses of Revelation.

Mentoring Relationships

As we begin our discussion of prophetic mentoring, let me place this issue in its proper context. Wherever I travel in the world, there is a severe shortage of mature prophets. This shortage is critical because prophets, along with apostles, are one of the foundational ministries through which the church is built. If this crippling problem is to be remedied, we must address the issue of prophetic development. In order to do this, we will examine both the school model and the discipleship approach.

The School Model

The first prophetic school was founded under the ministry of the prophet Samuel at Ramah (1 Sam. 19:18-24). These schools also seemed to flourish under the ministries of Elijah and Elisha, where we see schools or groups of prophets in the cities of Bethel and Jericho (2 Kings 2). Although Samuel's motivation for establishing the school of the prophets is never stated in Scripture, it is clear from 1 Samuel 3:1 that Samuel was born into a period of time where prophets and prophecy were rare: *The boy Samuel ministered before the LORD under Eli. In those days the word of the LORD was rare; there were not many visions.*

If Eli's inept mentoring of Samuel was any indicator (1 Sam. 3), this shortage stemmed, at least in part, from an inadequate process of identifying and developing new prophets. These were the needs I believe Samuel was seeking to address when he founded his school. Although the specific curriculum and operation of the school of the prophets is never spelled out in Scripture, there are a number of principles and applications which can be extracted for our present day situation.

Principle 1: **The schools were under the leadership of a mature, recognized prophet** (1 Sam. 19:20).

This is a critical point, because it takes a mature prophet to effectively develop other prophets. Furthermore, it is important that a prophet have a recognized ministry because, like many other institutions, students are drawn to prophetic schools through the people who lead them. This recognition is also important within the informal setting of prophetic training, due to the fact that the lead prophet's reputation becomes the credentials for those who have been trained.

Principle 2: **The student prophet (or child of the prophets) prophesied under the leadership of seasoned prophets.**

In my own experience, I have found that it is not enough to merely teach on prophecy in prophetic schools. The student prophets must have practical, hands-on experience. Two of the things I have done are as follows: First, in order to develop young prophets' skill in prophesying over individuals, I bring in volunteers who will allow immature prophets to minister to them. After every prophecy, the volunteers give their candid, public evaluation of the accuracy, clarity, and spirit of the prophecy. Second, when teaching how to preach prophetically, I give the young prophets the name of a church with which I am familiar. I give them a few days to receive and prepare a prophetic exhortation or message for that church. They then give it front of the whole class and I evaluate it.

Principle 3: **In the supernaturally-charged atmosphere of a prophetic school, the spirit of prophecy can become so prevalent that it becomes very easy to prophesy.**

For example, the anointing on Samuel's prophetic school was so strong that even the apostate King Saul and his murderous servants fell to the ground and begin to prophesy (1 Sam. 19:20-24). We must not forget, however, that the prophetic accessibility created within this divinely-charged atmosphere is both helpful and dangerous. It is helpful, because in this atmosphere genuine, emerging prophets can gain the confidence and clarity they need to build a solid foundation of faith. It can be dangerous because people who are not really prophets can come under a tremendous prophetic anointing. These divine anomalies can create a false sense of calling and destiny unless they are maturely evaluated.

Principle 4: **The prophetic schools of the Old Testament were more than just a three-day conference or six-month training school.**

The students lived together in a prophetic community (2 Kings 4:38-41; 6:1-7). Although I am not advocating a return to the prophetic communities of the Old Testament, it is critical that we realize the time it takes to truly raise up prophets.

Principle 5: **In 2 Kings 9:1-13, we find that maturing prophets from the prophetic schools were sent out to minister.**

In my own experience, I have found that emerging prophets must be given increasing levels of responsibility and ministry. Normally there are at least three stages within this process:

> *Stage 1:* Student prophets accompany me on ministry trips. As I prophesy over individuals, they write down everything they are hearing. After the meeting, we compare what they were hearing with what I said, as well as evaluating their revelation on its own merits.

> *Stage 2:* As they mature, I allow the students to prophesy over people with me. This allows me to examine both the level of their revelation and the style and manner in which they presented it.

> *Stage 3:* Students are sent out under my authority to prophesy and minister in churches. Initially, I arrange the trips for them. The host pastors understand that they are still learning and make allowances for that. The students are accountable to both the host pastor and to me for the content and the spirit of their prophecies. Hopefully, as they mature, the students' gifts will begin to create opportunities for their ministry without my help.

The Discipleship Approach

As we talk about mentoring relationships in the prophetic, it is clear that we must go beyond the school model and begin to talk about prophetic discipleship. Prophetic schools are excellent places for emerging prophets to be identified and educated. However, unless older prophets are willing to disciple younger prophets, I am convinced that we will never raise up the number of world-changing prophets that this incredible hour requires. Let's take a moment now to examine the power of these relationships in the lives of Elijah and Elisha.

Elijah and Elisha

Elijah's ministry was at its height. Fire had fallen from heaven, 400 prophets of Baal were killed, and the drought which had ravaged the land for years was ended. It had been the most miraculous display of power seen in the nation of Israel for hundreds of years. Yet, Jezebel was still on her throne threatening to murder him. Weakened by his battles on the mountain, he ran for his life into the desert. Like anyone who has given their best and found out it was not enough, Elijah wanted to quit. God's answer to him would change both his life and the life of his whole nation:

The LORD said to him, "Go back the way you came, and go to the Desert of Damascus. When you get there, anoint Hazael king over Aram. Also, anoint Jehu son of Nimshi king over Israel, and anoint Elisha son of Shaphat from Abel Meholah to succeed you as prophet. Jehu will put to death any who escape the sword of Hazael, and Elisha will put to death any who escape the sword of Jehu. Yet I reserve seven thousand in Israel—all whose knees have not bowed down to Baal and all whose mouths have not kissed him" (I Kings 19:15-18).

Simply stated, "Elijah, go back and face her; but this time, do it differently. Raise up other leaders, and make disciples. Above all else, reproduce yourself!"

I believe these same words are ringing in the ears of prophets around the world today. Like me, they have discovered that no matter how anointed they are, it is not enough. If they are to change the nations they love, they must reproduce themselves. Not just once, but again, and again, and again!

As Elijah returned to his mission, two things stand out: First, the man God chose to replace him was not a student in the school of the prophets. He was a young businessman from Abel Meholah—named Elisha. Second, Elijah never enrolled Elisha in the school of the prophets. He personally discipled and trained him. In both the selection of Elisha and the way God chose to train him, there are a number of principles that can be extracted and applied to our own day:

Principle 1: **Elisha was an unlikely candidate.**

The man called to replace Elijah was not a student in one of Israel's burgeoning prophetic schools. He was a young businessman. What a shock this must have been to Elijah. Surely God could have found an outstanding candidate among the scores of young prophets emerging out of the schools in Bethel and Jericho. After all, some of them had been faithfully training for years. Yet, God in His wisdom knew better. Elisha's anointing and gifting would eventually grow beyond Elijah's as he continued the prophetic work that his mentor had begun.

This principle is directly applicable to our own time, because I believe God is currently calling forth the greatest number of prophets and miracle workers in the church's history. Like Elisha, however, many of these men and women will be called out of demographics, professions, and nations that are not traditional sources for emerging prophets and prophetesses. Whether they are children with a lifetime of ministry ahead of them, or broken people from a poverty-stricken area of our world, prophets must be open to God's divine choosing in this critical hour.

Principle 2: **Elijah chose discipleship over a prophetic school.**

When faced with the choice of how to train the man who would replace him, Elijah chose to personally disciple and mentor Elisha instead of enrolling him in one of the prophetic schools. Although prophetic schools had their place, Elijah realized that it would take concentrated, personal discipleship to train the man who would replace him.

It is no different today. No matter how anointed the prophets are who lead them, prophetic "activation" sessions, conferences, and schools are not sufficient to raise up the caliber of prophets the church so desperately needs. This need will only be filled when mature prophets in the body of Christ give themselves to discipling and mentoring the next generation of prophets.

Principle 3: **Elisha had to realize that God had called him.**

After Elijah threw his mantle on him, Elisha ran after him shouting, *"Elijah, let me kiss my father and mother good-by, and then I will come back to you." Elijah answered, "Go back! What have I done to you?"* (1 Kings 19:19).

This was more than a simple release from a crotchety old prophet to tell his parents good-bye. In his question, Elijah was asking Elisha if he knew what had just happened to him. Did Elisha realize that God Himself was calling him through the ministry of the man who had just cast a mantle on his shoulders? This was critical, because even the hero worship and respect he felt for Elijah would not be enough to sustain him during the long and arduous period of training that lay ahead of him. He had to realize God's calling.

The same is true for prophetic mentoring relationships today. If prophetic students do not realize it was God who called them—both to the prophetic ministry and also to the person who is training them—they will never make it! Whether it is an offense, discouragement, or a misunderstanding, something will come to test the assurance of their calling.

Principle 4: **Elisha set out to follow Elijah and became his attendant or servant** (1 Kings 19:21).

His job description is even more carefully spelled out in 2 Kings 3:11: *"Elisha, son of Shaphat is here. He used to pour water on the hands of Elijah."*

That's right; Elisha did not become Elijah's co-prophet, peer, or partner. He became his butler, or servant. Although this aspect of Elisha's training may be hard for us to comprehend, Elijah realized this wealthy young farmer would never be a successful prophet until he learned the humility and brokenness of a servant.

The application of this principle is sorely needed in the church today. If emerging prophets to not develop the graces of humility, patience, and servanthood, they will never be qualified to safely exercise the dynamite of God's prophetic power.

Practically speaking, I would never train any person for the prophetic ministry who is not willing to humbly serve in their local church, no matter how menial the task asked of them seems. Furthermore, if an emerging prophet is unwilling to receive the correction and input that this depth of discipleship entails, I will not train them. The body of Christ has been hurt enough by insecure, arrogant prophets who claim that only God can correct them or even speak to them.

Principle 5: **Elisha's gifting was tested.**

After Elisha ask for a double portion of Elijah's anointing, Elijah told him his request would be answered if he could *"...see him when he was taken"* (2 Kings 2:10). What did Elijah mean by this? The answer is simple, yet profound. If Elijah had been truly called to be a prophet and had faithfully developed his gift while being mentored, he would see Elijah being taken to heaven. If he could not perceive this supernatural event, he was neither a prophet nor a faithful disciple. Whichever be the case, the mantle of the double portion would not be his.

Like Elisha, all prophetic students will eventually have their gifts tested. Whether they are standing in front of a room full of people who need prophecies, or ministering to a church in crisis, their day will come. They will either pick up the mantle like Elisha did, or wander around in confusion like the fifty prophets who searched for Elijah for three days.

In my own experience, I have found that no matter how much I care for the young prophets I have mentored, there is not much I can do for them when this moment comes. Either their gift will make room for them, or it won't. That is why it is so vital that prophets select the right disciples and mentor them carefully.

Principle 6: **Elijah was a spiritual father.**

When Elijah saw Elisha being taken to heaven, he cried out, "My father, my father." This simply illustrates the fact that Elijah was more than a mentor and a teacher to Elisha; he was a father. In fact, when Elisha requested to inherit a double portion of Elijah's anointing, he was simply asking for his rights as the firstborn son.

The place of fathering in prophetic mentoring cannot be minimized. Elijah, like any mature natural or spiritual father, was not threatened when Elisha asked for twice the anointing that he had. He wanted his prophetic son to surpass him. It is no different with the prophets I have fathered and mentored. There is nothing I would not do for them. When they succeed, I succeed. If we are to successfully raise up the next generation of prophets, these attitudes must burn in our hearts.

Before we finish our examination of prophetic mentoring, however, lets take a moment to discuss the relationship between Elisha and Gehazi.

Elisha and Gehazi

In 2 Kings 13:21, we find the amazing story of the dead man who was thrown into Elisha's tomb. When his corpse touched Elisha's bones, he was immediately raised from the dead. Although I marvel at the supernatural power portrayed in this story, I also have to wonder why there was still anointing in Elisha's bones? Could it be that, unlike Elijah, he had not passed his prophetic mantle on to anyone else before he died. If this was true, what had happened?

It seems clear from Scripture such as 2 Kings 4:6-21, Gehazi was the man Elisha was training to be his replacement. He was obviously more than just a faithful servant because Elijah gave him his rod and sent him to raise the Shuanmmite's son from the dead. Tragically, when he attempted to profit from Elisha's healing of Naaman, he was cursed with leprosy for the rest of his life. Whether Elisha ever attempted to personally disciple another prophet or not, we will never know. Let's take a moment now to extract a few principles from this tragic story:

Principle 1: **Although prophetic schools have their place, prophetic anointing is imparted through personal discipleship and mentoring.**

Out of the scores of prophets who were part of prophetic

schools or companies during that time, none of them received Elisha's anointing.

Principle 2: **Character development is critical.**
Gehazi was not disqualified for his lack of anointing. His destruction came through his lack of character.

Principle 3: **History is filled with prophets like Elisha, who have died without passing their mantle to another prophet.**
Although there is still life in their books and tapes, many prophets have left no one on the earth who has an anointing equal or greater than their own.

One of the crying needs of our hour is for prophets and prophetesses who will be willing to personally mentor the next generation of prophetic ministers. When I reflect on my own life and ministry, I know I would not have the prophetic anointing I have today if it were not for prophets such as Bobby Martz, Fred Herzog, and Keith Hazel. Each one of these men carefully mentored a different aspect of the prophetic anointing in my life. My prayer is that God will raise up more prophets like them as we seek to bring forth the next generation of prophets and prophetesses.

Ministry Relationships

The last aspect of prophetic relationships we will discuss are what I call ministry relationships. I have found that when prophets work together in teams, the anointing on their lives increases exponentially. Although Scripture does not go into the specifics of these relationships, there are at least two prophetic teams in Scripture from which we can make some observations and applications: the teams of Judas and Silas, and the two witnesses of Revelation.

Judas and Silas

After the Jerusalem Council, the apostles sent Judas and Silas, who were prophets, to deliver the Council's conclusions to the church at Antioch. Their visit to this church is described in Acts 15:22-23; 30-32:

Then the apostles and elders, with the whole church, decided to choose some of their own men and send them to Antioch with Paul and Barnabas. They chose Judas (called Barsabbas) and Silas, two men who were leaders among the brothers. With them they sent the following letter...

The men were sent off and went down to Antioch, where they gathered the church together and delivered the letter. The people read it and were glad for its encouraging message. Judas and Silas, who themselves were prophets, said much to encourage and strengthen the brothers.

From this passage, we can draw two important principles of prophetic team ministry:

Principle 1: **The definition and order provided by apostolic authority plays a vital role in the development of the atmosphere necessary for successful prophetic teamwork.**

It is clear from Acts 15:22 that Judas and Silas were sent under the authority of an apostolic team. If my own experience is any indicator, most prophets do work better together when they are under apostolic authority.

Whether it is the eccentricities and peculiarities particular to this office, or the insecurities and pride with which all leaders wrestle, many prophets (outside of mentoring relationships) do not naturally work well in teams. Left to themselves, leadership among prophets is normally decided by the variables of age, reputation, who scheduled the meeting, or "presumed" anointing. Although these factors count for something, many times they are no more than a recipe for chaos. With apostolic definition, however, prophetic leaders or senior prophets can be recognized. When this has been done, it is much easier to create the atmosphere necessary for successful prophetic team-work.

Principle 2:   **Prophetic anointing increases exponentially when prophets work together in teams.**

According to Acts 15:33, the church at Antioch was greatly encouraged by the words spoken through Judas and Silas. Although Luke does not elaborate on how they ministered together, I believe that there are at least four reasons for the divine synergism that can be created through prophetic team-work. The first two reasons are found in 1 Corinthians 12:4-6: *There are different kinds of gifts, but the same Spirit. There are different kinds of service, but the same Lord. There are different kinds of working, but the same God works all of them in all men.*

1. Gift combinations. The different spiritual gifts of every team member, when used in divine concert with one another, can dramatically increase a prophetic team's effectiveness. Let me give you an example of this from my own life. One of the prophets I enjoy working with is John Rohr. John has been uniquely gifted in emotional healing and deliverance. When we are prophesying together over individuals, God uses me to identify deep areas of pain in peoples lives through the word of knowledge. This enables the gift of healing, which operates through John, to work more effectively. The divine combination of these two gifts has produced healing and breakthroughs in countless lives.

2. Operational combinations. Even as there are different gifts, so each gift can operate or work differently in each person who has that gift. Within the prophetic office, there are at least three distinct workings or operations. Although most prophets can operate in at least a measure of all these prophetic spheres (workings), they are typically stronger or more fluent in one of them:

♦ *Prophetic Seers.* This is the visionary operation of the prophetic office. Prophets who operate as seers have an unique ability to see into the invisible realm. As they mature, their lives are marked by a steady stream of visionary revelation.

♦ *Prophetic Presbyters.* These prophets are uniquely gifted in personal prophecy. Whenever they pray for people, these prophets are supernaturally enabled to speak the prophetic word of the Lord to those whom they are ministering.

♦ *Prophetic Preachers.* Prophets who are anointed to bring the prophetic word of the Lord to churches, cities, and nations through preaching and teaching.

When a prophetic team— which has all three of these spheres or operations represented—moves in concert, the results (in a church or a conference) can be incredible! For example, while the prophet gifted to preach prophetically is speaking, the team member who is the most fluent in prophetic presbytery can be preparing to lead the team in personal prophecy. Meanwhile, the most gifted seer on the team is receiving the revelatory insight necessary for the team to minister effectively. This type of teamwork has the ability to dramatically lift the level of prophetic anointing experienced by every team member.

3. The power of unity. According to Psalm 133, God commands a blessing on unity. Part of this blessing comes through an increase in the Holy Spirit's anointing and power:

How good and pleasant it is when brothers live together in unity! It is like precious oil poured on the head, running down on the beard, running down on Aaron's beard, down upon the collar of his robes. It is as if the dew of Hermon were falling on Mount Zion. For there the LORD bestows his blessing, even life forevermore.

Like every other area of ministry, this blessing can be experienced through prophetic teamwork. The cost, however, is heavy. In my own experience, I have found that it takes true humility and deep brokenness for a group of prophets to create the kind of harmony and unity that God will truly bless. Yet, despite the cost, once a team has experienced the release of divine favor and anointing that this blessing brings, they will pay any price to keep it.

4. Prophetic drafting. In bicycle racing, there is a concept called drafting. When a bicyclist is drafting, he rides behind another bicyclist who breaks wind resistance for him. This allows the bicyclist who is drafting to conserve his energy in preparation for sprints and other more arduous portions of the course. This concept is so effective in team racing, different bicyclists will take turns riding in front, so the rest of the team can draft.

The same concept can be directly applied to prophetic team ministry. For example, when I am prophesying over individuals with a group of other prophets, we draft all the time. The first prophet to speak typically breaks through any resistance barriers. While that person is prophesying, the rest of the team waits on God for a word that will enable them to sprint ahead—through the openness that the first prophecy is creating. Furthermore, as the revelation they are receiving is confirmed by the words of the first prophet, the team's confidence also grows. As this process continues, the words normally increase in clarity and depth.

One of the prophets with whom I enjoy drafting the most is Jim Critcher. Unlike John Rohr and me, our power together does not come from the differences in our giftings; it comes from the similarities. Both of us operate consistently in the word of knowledge. No matter who goes first, both the accuracy and the clarity of our gifts grow when we work together. For example, when either Jim or I seemingly gets out of revelation, the one of us not ministering simply begins to minister. At that point, the prophetic ministry will either continue in the same vein at a deeper level, or a whole new revelatory vein will be opened.

This type of prophetic drafting is possible for two reasons. First, we have the ability to both wait on the Lord and to reflect on what the other person is ministering while they are prophesying. Second, while one of us is prophesying, the confidence and faith of the person not prophesying grows as they hear the very revelation they were pondering being expressed under the anointing.

The Two Witnesses of Revelation

Whether it is gift or operational combinations, the power of unity or prophetic drafting, prophetic teamwork brings a fresh release of prophetic revelation and power to both the church and the world we have been called to win. Probably the greatest example of this can be found in what I believe will be history's greatest prophetic team – the two witnesses of Revelation. One of the most unique passages of Scripture is John's account of the ministry of the two witnesses in Revelation 11:3-12:

"...And I will give power to my two witnesses, and they will prophesy for 1,260 days, clothed in sackcloth." These are the two olive trees and the two lampstands that stand before the Lord of the earth. If anyone tries to harm them, fire comes from their mouths and devours their enemies. This is how anyone who wants to harm them must die. These men have power to shut up the sky so that it will not rain during the time they are prophesying; and they have power to turn the waters into blood and to strike the earth with every kind of plague as often as they want.

Now when they have finished their testimony, the beast that comes up from the Abyss will attack them, and overpower and kill them. Their bodies will lie in the street of the great city, which is figuratively called Sodom and Egypt, where also their Lord was crucified. For three and a half days men from every people, tribe, language and nation will gaze on their bodies and refuse them burial. The inhabitants of the earth will gloat over them and will celebrate by sending each other gifts, because these two prophets had tormented those who live on the earth.

But after the three and a half days a breath of life from God entered them, and they stood on their feet, and terror struck those who saw them. Then they heard a loud voice from heaven saying to them, "Come up here." And they went up to heaven in a cloud, while their enemies looked on.

As to the identity of these two powerful prophets, there are many opinions. A number of Christians speculate that they are Moses and Elijah, while others believe they represent a group of Christians. Although it is impossible to be sure, I personally believe they are Moses and Elijah. Whether I am right or not, however, we definitely have one of the most powerful examples of prophetic ministry in all of Scripture. Two principles of prophetic team ministry that can be drawn from this passage are as follows:

Principle 1: **When mature prophets are willing to walk in team ministry, there will be an incredible manifestation of God's power in their lives.**

The team of Moses and Elijah will be marked by incredible signs and wonders and an amazing flow of prophecy. I am convinced that this type of teamwork between mature prophets is critical, if we are ever going to impact our increasingly pagan culture.

Principle 2: **As mature prophetic teams release the revelation and power of the Holy Spirit, the cultures, cities, and nations of the world will be radically impacted.**

According to John, the impact of Moses and Elijah on the world was so terrifying that their death created a global sensation.

To Summarize...

We live in an hour of incredible hunger for supernatural reality. This hunger will either be satisfied by the deception and subterfuge of the enemy, through his minions, or by the supernatural power of our awesome God, through His servants. As witches, warlocks, shamans, and New Age practitioners become more and more accepted in our society, it is critical that we rise up to meet this challenge. This challenge will not be overcome by apologetics and intellectual disputation alone. It will take the full release of God's supernatural power through the lives and ministries of both apostles and prophets to stem the tide of darkness that threatens to overwhelm our culture.

Let's take a moment now to summarize some of the critical principles we discussed in this chapter:

1. There is a critical need for prophets, both in the body of Christ and our in culture.

2. Although prophetic schools have an important role to play in meeting this need, discipleship and mentoring are at the very essence of raising up a new generation of prophets. Therefore, it is critical that every mature prophet find and disciple one or more emerging prophets.

3. Prophetic training and discipleship must include both practical prophetic training and serious character development.

4. The anointing on prophets increases exponentially when they work together in teams.

5. This increase in power and anointing is produced through gift and operational combinations, prophetic drafting, and the divine blessings God promises to those who walk in humility and unity.

6. Without the definition and authority of apostolic leadership, many prophets will never be able to walk in long-term prophetic ministry team relationships.

7. As our world continues to cry out for supernatural reality, God wants to bring a new level of anointing into the lives of His prophetic servants, to prepare them for the power encounters that are sure to come.

CHAPTER FOUR

THE RELATIONSHIP
AMONG APOSTLES

As God continues to raise up apostles in this hour, the issue of how they work together is becoming increasingly vital to the overall advance of God's kingdom. Some of the current thought on the issue suggests that every apostle should have their own family, or network, of churches. An example of this school of thought can be seen in C. Peter Wagner's excellent book, *Apostles and Prophets* (Regal Books). In his section on avoiding the return to denominationalism, Wagner makes the following statement:

"Multiply apostolic networks. When new apostles emerge within a given apostolic network, the founding apostle should release them and bless them in every way to start their own new networks. This avoids routinization because (1) it keeps the number of churches in each network at a manageable level, and (2) it provides first generation leadership for each new network" (p. 72).

Wisdom in Apostolic Release

Before we examine this model of apostolic ministry, let's take a moment to discuss the sociological concept of "routinization of charisma." Routinization comes from the word routinize, which means to become routine or habitual. The term routinization of charisma is used to describe a process in which an organization goes from charismatic (in the sociological sense of the word) leadership to bureaucratic leadership. This normally takes place when the organization's visionary founder dies and the followers or employees attempt to develop some form of bureaucratic structure to perpetuate their leader's "charisma" (a personal appeal or power that attracts people). From then on, new leaders are normally chosen through a process of democratic consensus.

Although, like Wagner, I believe God does call many apostles to birth their own family of churches, I am also convinced that this is not the only legitimate model. In fact, I believe if the one-apostle-per-network model is the only model of building apostolic networks perpetuated, the ability of the body of Christ to advance the kingdom of God around the world could be impaired. My reasons for this are as follows:

First, if this is the only model, young apostles, who are maturing within existing families of churches, will always feel the need to take the churches they have planted and start their own apostolic family. Even when this is done in the highest possible way, the existing family of churches is normally severely weakened, and the new family of churches needs years to build to the same level of maturity and resource that was lost. Furthermore, if all the parties involved in the release of a young apostle (and the churches he has planted) do not act with the utmost maturity and wisdom, this model, by its very nature, will breed division and strife. Unfortunately, in most cases, the parties involved do not use wisdom, and everyone concerned is affected by the division.

Second, if an apostolic family of churches continually releases all their emerging young apostles, the routinization of the parent organization's charisma is almost guaranteed. With all their young apostles gone, there will eventually be no visionary apostles left to lead the church family.

Third, if we do not develop a model of apostolic partnership involving mature apostles, laboring within the same family and believing for the same vision, we will miss a strategic key for the present harvest. I am convinced that when God finds a team like this, a group of mature apostles who have dealt with the issues of authority and territory, He brings an unprecedented release of His power and wisdom. If we are to experience this level of apostolic partnership, however, it is critical that we develop another model.

Although I myself am not an apostle, after decades of walking intimately with incredible apostles, I believe the three apostolic teams of the New Testament, the teams of Jesus, Peter, and Paul, provide an tremendous model for apostolic life and ministry. Each provides a set of principles that are worth examining.

The Apostolic Team of Jesus

As we examine the apostolic team of Jesus we find seven critical principles of apostolic partnership:

Principle 1: Anointed apostleship.
Therefore, holy brothers, who share in the heavenly call-

ing, fix your thoughts on Jesus, the apostle and high priest whom we confess (Heb 3:1).

Jesus was their apostle, and that says it all. He had the anointing and character necessary to draw, train, release, and lead the caliber of men necessary to apostolically change the world. It is the same today. Only a mature apostle who has been uniquely anointed by God can develop and maintain a team of apostles.

Even as there are pastors gifted by God to build megachurches and lead a team of pastors, so there are apostles who have received the measure of the apostolic gift necessary to lead other apostles in a family of churches. Whether it was the teams led by Jesus, Peter, or Paul, or the teams God is building on the earth today, the concept of senior apostleship is at the very essence of building strong apostolic families of churches.

Principle 2: **Passion for the harvest.**

Jesus went through all the towns and villages, teaching in their synagogues, preaching the good news of the kingdom and healing every disease and sickness. When he saw the crowds, he had compassion on them, because they were harassed and helpless, like sheep without a shepherd. Then he said to his disciples, "The harvest is plentiful but the workers are few. Ask the Lord of the harvest, therefore, to send out workers into his harvest field" (Matt 9:35-38).

In this passage, we find that Jesus carried a deep sense of the immensity of the harvest; this was His motivation to train and release the next generation of apostles. When I consider the apostles with whom I have ministered over the last 27 years, this passion for the harvest has marked all of their lives. One of the men whose life exemplifies this passion is Jim Marocco, the pastor of Maui First Assembly. I never cease to be amazed at his heart for the harvest. Whether it is lead-ing 6 a.m. prayer seven days a week, or planting churches throughout the islands of the world, his life is consumed with a vision for the harvest.

Principle 3: Observation of apostolic qualities.

One of those days Jesus went out to a mountainside to pray, and spent the night praying to God. When morning came, he called his disciples to him and chose twelve of them, whom he also designated apostles (Luke 6:12-13).

After a night of prayer, Jesus selected twelve of His lead-ers to serve as apostles. I believe His selection was based on two things: the witness of the Spirit He received from His Father (while praying), and the observation of the apostolic qualities He saw in their lives.

Although praying is obviously important, the process of observation is equally critical. Whether it is the office of an apostle (or any other office in the church), we do not ordain people into a church office simply because we have a sense that they will one day be walking in that office. We ordain them because they are already walking in a measure of the office. This is why the process of observing a person's life and ministry is so critical.

Principle 4: Public impartation of apostolic authority.

When morning came, he called his disciples to him and chose twelve of them, whom he also designated apostles (Luke 6:13).

He appointed twelve—designating them apostles—that they might be with him and that he might send them out to preach and to have authority to drive out demons (Mark 3:14-15).

[Jesus said to them] *"As you go, preach this message:*

'The kingdom of heaven is near.' Heal the sick, raise the dead, cleanse those who have leprosy, drive out demons. Freely you have received, freely give" (Matt 10:7-8).

In this principle, we find that Jesus set His designated apostles into their apostleship publicly. This setting, however, was more than just a religious formality. There was an actual impartation of miraculous power and apostolic authority. I believe we will begin to see more and more of this type of impartation as mature apostles demonstrate the miraculous in their lives and impart it to the next generation of apostles.

Principle 5: A specific mission.

He appointed twelve—designating them apostles—that they might be with him and that he might send them out to preach and to have authority to drive out demons (Mark 3:14-15).

This principle is simple, yet critical. He sent them on a specific mission. In my opinion, the application of this principle is vital to the development of apostles and the family of churches they serve. It is not enough to merely set a person into the office of an apostle. They must be set in for a specific purpose. When this is done, the apostolic gift on their life will mature and the family they serve will grow.

Principle 6: Strategic mission accountability.

The apostles gathered around Jesus and reported to him all they had done and taught (Mark 6:30).

The principle of strategic mission accountability is especially important in the development of the apostolic team. As the apostolic team members report the results of their mission, three things happen: One, younger team members gain wisdom from the feedback they receive. Two, fresh unity and synergism is created as the team hears the testimonies of its various members. Three, new ideas, strategies, and the faith to accomplish them is released as the whole team has the opportunity to respond to the reports they have received.

Before we examine the seventh principle, let me take a moment to illustrate the operation of these principles from my own experience. Over the last three years, I have watched some of the leaders in my own spiritual family step into their apostleship. This has happened for at least two reasons: First, our apostolic team leader, Rice Broocks, and a number of our other apostles have the anointing and character necessary to raise up new apostles. Second, the members of our apostolic team are actively believing God to raise up the apostolic leaders necessary to fulfill the mission He has given us as a family.

One of the men who has been stepping into his apostolic calling is a gifted evangelist. For years, we have seen apostolic potential in his life. Recently, while praying, Rice sensed that this man was called to lead our church planting efforts in New Zealand, Australia, and islands of the South Pacific. After sharing it with the apostolic team, he asked the evangelist, Ken Dew, if he was willing to be sent by the apostolic team to accomplish this mission. Although at the time it was not a burden on Ken's heart, he trusted Rice and rest of the apostolic team enough to seriously pray about it. When the Holy Spirit confirmed it in his heart, we assembled a team around him, set him in as team leader, and sent the entire team out. Today, after only a few months, there is a growing church, leaders are being trained, and new cities and nations are already being targeted. This is just one example out of many I could share with you which serve to illustrate the application of these critical principles.

Principle 7: **A designated successor.**
Jesus replied, "Blessed are you, Simon son of Jonah, for

this was not revealed to you by man, but by my Father in heaven. And I tell you that you are Peter, and on this rock I will build my church, and the gates of Hades will not overcome it. I will give you the keys of the kingdom of heaven; whatever you bind on earth will be bound in heaven, and whatever you loose on earth will be loosed in heaven" (Matt. 16:17-19).

"Simon, Simon, Satan has asked to sift you as wheat. But I have prayed for you, Simon, that your faith may not fail. And when you have turned back, strengthen your brothers" (Luke 22:31-32).

When they had finished eating, Jesus said to Simon Peter, "Simon son of John, do you truly love me more than these?" "Yes, Lord," he said, "you know that I love you." Jesus said, "Feed my lambs."

Again Jesus said, "Simon son of John, do you truly love me?" He answered, "Yes, Lord, you know that I love you." Jesus said, "Take care of my sheep."

The third time he said to him, "Simon son of John, do you love me?" Peter was hurt because Jesus asked him the third time, "Do you love me?" He said, "Lord, you know all things; you know that I love you." Jesus said, "Feed my sheep" (John 21:15-17).

From these passages, we find that Jesus prepared the disciples for His death by designating one of them to be His successor. It was not merely an organizational designation. Throughout the Gospels, it is clear that Jesus dealt with Peter more severely than all the other disciples. He had seen the leadership potential in Peter's life and was dealing with him accordingly. This dealing prepared Peter to receive the anointing he would need to lead the apostolic team Jesus had birthed. Furthermore, as we clearly see in the book of Acts, Jesus' careful selection and mentoring of Peter also kept the early church from routinizing. This is an important point, because I believe whenever God finds senior apostles who are willing to lead proactively—by carefully mentoring and grooming the apostles who will succeed them—routinization can be avoided.

Tragically many leaders today are more like Isaac than Jesus. If they choose a successor at all, they choose the wrong one. Like Isaac, who was blind to the hand of God on Jacob (because of tradition and his own affinity with Esau), they choose their successor based on seniority or personality. May God make us like Jesus, who looked beyond His deep affinity with John, and choose Peter to lead the team, even though he had been the hardest of all the apostles to train.

The Apostolic Team of Peter

The next model of apostolic relationships we will examine is the apostolic team of Peter. Let's take a moment now to examine some of the principles found in this amazing team.

Principle 1: **Senior apostleship.**

Then Peter stood up with the Eleven, raised his voice and addressed the crowd: "Fellow Jews and all of you who live in Jerusalem, let me explain this to you; listen carefully to what I say" (Acts 2:14).

Then Peter, filled with the Holy Spirit, said to them: "Rulers and elders of the people!" (Acts 4:8).

Peter and the other apostles replied: "We must obey God rather than men!" (Acts 5:29).

In the first few chapters of the book of Acts, it is clear Peter has received the anointing he needed to lead the apostolic team of Jesus into their God-given mission. As we see in these passages, the hopes of Jesus for Peter had been fulfilled. He was not only the spokesman for the team; he was their leader. Even though these men were his peers and friends, Peter would go on to successfully lead them for years. He had become like Jesus—what I will term a senior apostle—an apostle who has been uniquely gifted by God to lead other apostles into their God-given mission.

Think for a moment how amazing this was. Peter was leading men like Andrew, his own natural brother, who had brought him to the Lord; and John, who had been a disciple of John the Baptist. All the team had seen his pride and arrogance, and worse yet, they had all watched him deny Jesus three times. Yet, as his character was transformed through the greatest failures of his life, he received the mantle necessary to lead this extraordinary team of men.

This concept of senior apostleship is critical for this hour. Until we acknowledge the unique measure of the apostolic gift God places on the lives of some of His servants, we will never have teams of apostles coming into the divine synergism and effectiveness God has for them.

Principle 2: **The leadership core.**

In Matthew 17:1-2, we find that Peter was not the only of the apostles who Jesus was preparing for senior apostleship. Whether it was the Mount of Transfiguration or later in the Garden of Gethsemene (Mark 14:32-34), Jesus brought Peter, James, and John into the realities of what He was facing in order to prepare them for the mantle of leadership they would one day inherit.

Although Peter was clearly the leader, these three men, who had been friends for years, formed the leadership core of this apostolic team. John played a prominent role in the early chapters of the book of Acts, and he wrote five books of the Bible. After the deaths of Peter and Paul, he became the early church's senior apostle.

As for James the brother of John, his role is never clearly defined in the book of Acts. Based on the fact that he was singled out for execution by Herod in Acts 12:1-2, however, it seems safe to assume that he had a prominent place on the apostolic team. He was replaced by James the half brother of Jesus, who had a vital role to play in the Jerusalem Council of Acts 15 and was designated by Paul as one of the pillars of the church.

It is no different in the family of churches where God has placed me. Although Rice Broocks is the team leader, he shares the leadership of the team with two other senior apostles— Phil Bonasso and Steve Murrell. Although there are other strong apostolic men on the team (who are also senior apostles), these two men have been uniquely graced by God to help lead our team. Rice's willingness to make room for the giftings of these men, as well as for the other apostles on our team, has been critical. Our whole family of churches is strengthened by the fact that a number of apostolic gifts are being expressed on its leadership team.

In addition, the individual apostolic leaders on our team can find the place of expression they need for their own giftings and callings. This is critical because I am convinced strong apostolic leaders will never work together in a long-term team relationship unless they have room to express the callings and destinies God has given them.

Principle 3: Function and fields.

In my own experience, I have found that the apostolic giftings are normally expressed in two ways: function and field. For example, the apostle James is never presented in Scripture as a gifted evangelist or church planter. He did, however, have an incredible gift of apostolic government and leadership. During the Jerusalem Council (Acts 15), it was James, not Peter or Paul, who had the wisdom necessary to negotiate the doctrinal disputes which threatened to divide the   early church. Furthermore, even Peter, who was the team leader, submitted to the leadership of James while he was operating in his own God-given function.

As for apostolic fields, in Galatians 2:7-9 we find two apostolic teams who were able to define their relationship—based on an understanding of God-given fields:

On the contrary, they saw that I had been entrusted with the task of preaching the gospel to the Gentiles, just as Peter had been to the Jews. For God, who was at work in the ministry of Peter as an apostle to the Jews, was also at work in my ministry as an apostle to the Gentiles. James, Peter and John, those reputed to be pillars, gave me and Barnabas the right hand of fellowship when they recognized the grace given to me. They agreed that we should go to the Gentiles, and they to the Jews.

This concept of God-given fields is vital. We must not forget that God gives both individual apostles and apostolic teams specific fields. These fields can be either demographic or geographic. For example, on our team, Ron Lewis, the pastor of King's Park International Church in North Carolina, has been mightily used by God to lead our efforts in China. This gifted church planter has touched almost every province in one of the world's most strategic nations. On the other hand, Brett Fuller, pastor of Grace Covenant Church in northern Virginia, has been uniquely gifted to reach the inner cities of America. Whether it is Ron, Brett, or Steve Murrell, who oversees our efforts in Asia, every member of our team is given the room they need to lead within their God-given field or function. Although every team member is under the authority of the whole team, we do our best to respect their leadership within the field God has given them.

Principle 4: **Divine additions.**

Lastly, in the team led by Peter, we find the principle of divine additions. When I use the term divine additions, I am referring to the process through which God adds new members to a leadership team. In the case of the team led by Peter, it was clear (after the betrayal of Judas) that God desired to add another apostle to their team.

"For," said Peter, *"it is written in the book of Psalms, 'May his place be deserted; let there be no one to dwell in it,' and, 'May another take his place of leadership'"* (Acts 1:20). Unfortunately, instead of waiting on God to reveal His choice, they simply picked the best possible candidates from the their current ministry circles. Then they cast lots to obtain the final decision (Acts 1:21-26). Although much can be said about the casting of lots, this was definitely not the way that Jesus, who had spent all night in prayer over His selections, had chosen them.

Furthermore, I have wondered if Matthias was ever God's choice to fill the place vacated by Judas. Could it have been that Paul was the man called by God to join the church's founding apostolic team? My reasons for this speculation are as follows: First, Paul, like the original apostles, was directly called into apostleship by the Lord Jesus (Acts 9:1-6; 1 Cor. 9:1). Second, his apostleship to the Gentile world was acknowledged by the apostolic team led by Peter (Gal. 2:7-9). Third, Paul acknowledged the authority of the team led by Peter when the early church's unity was threatened (Acts 15). Fourth, Paul was called to Antioch by Barnabas, who was under the authority of Peter's team (Acts 11:22-26). This is important because Antioch was the church from which Paul was sent apostolically.

If my speculations are correct, why wasn't Paul ever made part of the team led by Peter? I believed it revolved around three things: his past, his person, and his purpose. Unlike the rugged Galileans, who had been called and trained by Jesus, Paul was a highly educated, cosmopolitan Jew. Worse yet was the fact that he had been the church's strongest critic and greatest persecutor before he was saved. These problems were compounded by Paul's sharp temperament and combative personality. He fought with Barnabas, publicly rebuked Peter, and even referred to the big three (Peter, James, and John) sarcastically in his letter to the Galatians when he wrote, *"James, Peter and John, those reputed to be pillars,"* (Gal. 2:9, bold added).

Finally, after fourteen years of watching his ministry, they acknowledged his apostleship, and gave into his care the very field they had never really wanted in the first place – the Gentile world. The rest is history. Paul's team took the lead in obeying the mandate of Christ to reach the whole world.

What lessons can we draw from these speculations? First, we must be willing to allow God to add those to our leadership teams who are not from our immediate spiritual families. Second, at times we will have to overcome personality differences (and even past difficulties) in order to partner with the people with whom God has called us to walk. Third, many times the fulfillment of our God-given mandate is contingent upon our willingness to find and receive the right one (or ones) into our leadership teams.

Furthermore, even if my speculations about Paul's relationship with the apostolic team led by Peter are not correct, (and they may not be), this story provides a model for how to release emerging apostles into their destiny. Although there were tensions between Paul and Peter's apostolic team, Peter, James, and John blessed Paul's ministry and released him into the harvest God had given him.

This is a crucial point. If a member of the apostolic team

feels it is time to leave the team in order to start their own family or network of churches, it is critical that the team member's release be handled with the highest levels of integrity and maturity. Even if the process is painful, we should never forget that team membership is a voluntary association. Members are free to leave without being stigmatized as being either disloyal or a covenant breaker. This does not mean, however, in cases where there has been divisiveness or lack of integrity, that you simply ignore it. There are times where loving confrontation is part of the process.

The Apostolic Team of Paul

In addition to the principles outlined above, there are two additional principles we can glean from looking at the apostolic team of Paul.

Principle 1: **The art of appealing.**
First, although he could be combative and sharp, Paul learned the art of appealing. Examples of this skill can found throughout his letters:

I appeal to you, brothers, in the name of our Lord Jesus Christ, that all of you agree with one another so that there may be no divisions among you and that you may be perfectly united in mind and thought (1 Cor. 1:10).

By the meekness and gentleness of Christ, I appeal to you— I, Paul, who am "timid" when face to face with you, but "bold" when away! I beg you that when I come I may not have to be as bold as I expect to be toward some people who think that we live by the standards of this world (2 Cor. 10:1-2).

Therefore, although in Christ I could be bold and order you to do what you ought to do, yet I appeal to you on the basis of love. I then, as Paul—an old man and now also a prisoner of Christ Jesus—I appeal to you for my son Onesimus, who became my son while I was in chains (Phile. 1:8-10).

Although Paul was appealing to those who were under his authority, this skill is also vital in peer relationships and when dealing with those over us in the Lord.

When a person is communicating through an appeal, the following characteristics will be present: First, they are basing their desire to be heard on relationship, not on position. Whether it is the common relationship that they (and the person they are appealing to) share with Christ, or their history with one another, relationship is the foundation of their appeal. Second, the tenor of their appeal is never argumentative or dogmatic. There is always an attitude of meekness and gentleness. By this, I mean in their very attitude and demeanor, they are communicating both an openness to discuss their appeal and even a willingness to admit they are wrong.

I have found that this skill is vital in maintaining peer relationships within apostolic team on which I serve. In fact, we almost wear out the word appeal. I cannot count the times I have heard one team member say to another, "I appeal to you." Obviously, this is more than verbiage. On our team, we appeal to one another because we believe the relationships God has given us are more important than winning an argument or defending our opinions. I am convinced that this attitude is a potent antidote to the argumentative pride and dogmatism that have destroyed so many team relationships.

Principle 2: **Releasing younger apostles.**

Lastly, Paul, like Jesus, had the ability to discern and develop the apostolic gift in younger people. Whether it was Titus appointing elders (Titus 1:5) or sending Timothy to the church in Corinth (1 Cor. 4:17), Paul was continually releasing young apostles into their apostolic destiny.

It is also important to note, however, that Titus and Timothy were not attempting to establish their own network or family of churches. Titus and Timothy continued to labor with the Apostle Paul on the team he was leading. Yet, even when these young apostles were released into their apostolic ministry, they continued to build within the spiritual family that was led by Paul.

To Summarize...

Although God does call many apostles to lead their own network or family of churches, it is clear from our study of the apostolic teams of Jesus, Peter, and Paul, that it is not the only legitimate model. In fact, the model most clearly presented in the New Testament is one in which teams of apostles build families of churches together under the leadership of a senior apostle or a group of senior apostles. If we are to experience this quality of apostolic life and ministry, however, the following principles will be very important:

1. In order to develop and maintain teams of apostles, we must acknowledge both the existence and importance of senior apostles.

2. Every apostle on the team should be given a specific field or function. This principle becomes even more critical on teams where more than one senior apostle are working together.

3. A priority should be set on discerning and developing younger apostles.

4. Rising apostles need a specific mission for which

they are held accountable.

5. God, at times, will make surprising additions to the apostolic teams on which we serve. Whether these mature apostles are from outside of our immediate spiritual families or even our spiritual comfort zones, we must remain open to these divine additions.

6. Without the biblical skill of appealing and the development of the attitudes on which it is founded, strong apostles will never be able to walk in team relationships.

7. In order to build a spiritual family that will last more than one generation, it is critical that the senior apostles on a team develop and eventually designate the ones who will one day replace them.

8. If a member of the apostolic team feels it is time to leave the team in order to start their own family or network of churches, it is critical that this team member's release be handled with the highest levels of integrity and maturity.

The Heart of a Leader

Before I close this chapter, let me comment on one last issue. No matter how many models we examine, there are certain attitudes that must be dealt with in the heart of a leader. These attitudes are found in Luke 4:5-7:

The devil led him up to a high place and showed him in an instant all the kingdoms of the world. And he said to him, "I will give you all their authority and splendor, for it has been given to me, and I can give it to anyone I want to. So if you worship me, it will all be yours.""

As you can see, when Jesus was brought into the second level of temptation, it was not about the basic battles with lust that every person faces. He was led up to a high place and offered territory (kingdoms), authority, and splendor.

It is no different with us today. When we come into a higher place of leadership within the kingdom of God, we will face the temptation to have our own exclusive territory, to be our own authority, and to bask in the seeming splendor these things bring. Whether it is an apostle who desires to walk in team relationships, or one who simply needs help in the field God has assigned, these are the issues with which they must deal.

In my own experience, I have found that there are many leaders who articulate the need for team relationships, account-ability, and authority. Tragically, there are few who ever really experience it. What are the reasons for this incongruence? Although many reasons could be examined, one of the main reasons involves the pride and insecurity with which every leader wrestles in the depth of their hearts.

Simply stated, whether it is from wounding or pride, some leaders' need for their own territory and their own authority outweighs their intrinsic need for the protection, authority, and fulfillment that can be found through relating to other apostolic leaders. May all of us, therefore, rise above the in-security, pride, and fear that besets our souls, so we can experience everything God has for us in our ministries, mar-riages, and families.

CHAPTER FIVE

APOSTOLIC TEAMS AND THE SENIOR PASTOR

O ne of the most critical relationships in the body of Christ today is the relationship between senior pastors and the apostolic team. Before I tell you why I believe this to be true, let me define the term apostolic team. An apostolic team is a group of leaders who have been formed into a team, under the authority of an apostle, for the purpose of planting and governing churches. These teams primarily consist of apostles and prophets; however, evangelists, pastors, and teachers can also function apostolically.

In order to be as cogent as possible, I have divided this chapter into two sections. In the first section, we will discuss the importance of the apostolic team in the life of the senior pastor. In the second section, some of the impediments to this relationship will be examined.

The Importance of Apostolic Teams in the Life of a Senior Pastor

Although we discussed the vital role of apostles and prophets in Chapter One, there are a number of other reasons that relating to an apostolic team is important to the life of a senior pastor. Among the most important of these are accountability, authority, association, assignments, and advancement.

Reason 1: Accountability

The first reason is the issue of accountability; every leader needs someone who will look them in the eye and ask them about both the state of their own life and the condition of their family and ministry. How many leaders could have been saved through the simple application of accountability? Although peer accountability among pastors and leaders is both biblical and desirable, accountability without some form of authority is in reality no accountability at all.

Reason 2: Authority

That brings us to the second purpose of apostolic team in the life of a senior pastor – authority. Although this subject can be controversial, it is clearly a biblical issue:

Obey your leaders and submit to their authority. They keep watch over you as men who must give an account. Obey them so that their work will be a joy, not a burden, for that would be of no advantage to you (Heb. 13:17).

Authority, however, is not just for the people we are leading; it's also for us. Whether it was the authority Jesus exercised with the apostles He was training, or the authority Paul and John assumed with the leaders and churches under their oversight, the fact that leaders need authority in their lives is clear in Scripture. For authority to be properly exercised, however, wisdom is needed. In my own spiritual family, we have found the following parameters to be helpful:

1. Authority should be defined.

Within the Morning Star family, the areas have been clearly defined in writing where the apostolic team has authority in the life of a church or leader. For example, in the case of a serious church division or immorality in the life of a leader, the apostolic team is the final authority.

2. Submission is voluntary.

Leaders in the Morning Star Family freely submit to the authority God has placed in their lives. It is never a matter of coercion or pressure. Furthermore, although we believe in committed relationships, we realize that not all relationships will last forever. If a leader no longer feels called to walk with us, that person is not stigmatized as a "Jonah" or a covenant breaker. They can leave with a blessing. We know that there are many other incredible families within the family of God.

3. Authorities should be under authority.

Every apostle in the Morning Star family is accountable to the apostolic team. Even Rice Broocks, as team leader, willingly submits his decisions and life to the authority of the apostolic team's executive council (a core of senior apostles who provide direction and oversight for the whole team). This type of accountability is critical, because each leader in the Morning Star world knows that if they come into conflict or disagreement with any member of the apostolic team, they always have a place of appeal.

4. Pastoral authority flows both structurally and relationally.

Although the whole apostolic team has carefully de-lineated spheres of authority in every local church, we do not have regional apostles (or bishops). Every senior pastor and leader is free to discover the God-given relational links within the Morning Star family they and their churches or ministries need. In some cases these links have been formed through the years of discipleship and training they received while being prepared for the ministry. In other cases, where a minister has been adopted into our family, these links are formed supernaturally as leaders fellowship and receive ministry from the various members of the apostolic team.

On the other hand, as much as we value relational authority, we also realize that God may choose to exercise structural authority in our lives without relationship. For example, Paul had never visited the church in Rome, yet he exercised apostolic authority in the life of that church:

I long to see you so that I may impart to you some spiritual gift to make you strong—that is, that you and I may be mutually encouraged by each other's faith. I do not want you to be unaware, brothers, that I planned many times to come to you (but have been prevented from doing so until now) in order that I might have a harvest among you, just as I have had among the other Gentiles (Rom. 1:11-13).

It is no different for a pastor. Many times as a senior pastor, I had to exercise spiritual authority in the life of a person or persons I hardly knew. Although relationship would have made it easier, it would not have made it anymore legitimate. This distinction is critical, because in a culture desperately crying out for relationship, many people have made relationship a prerequisite for authority. Although relationships can be incredible, we must never forget the basis for spiritual authority is the Word of God, not relationships.

Yet, even when exercised within the parameters I have mentioned, the exercise of authority can be a painful thing, because at times it involves confrontation. Although many senior leaders have learned the skill of biblical confrontation, typically they are better at confronting than at being confronted themselves. In my own life and ministry, I have found that I have never outgrown the need for loving, biblical confrontation. Time and time again, my life and ministry have been shaped by the words and counsel of the prophets and apostles whom I have asked to speak into my life.

One of the reasons I believe the ability to receive truth from other leaders is so important is found in Ephesians 6:14: *Stand firm then, with the belt of truth buckled around your waist, with the breastplate of righteousness in place.*

In my opinion, the truth Paul is speaking about is not just the truth of God's Word. It is the truth about our lives, families, and ministries. Furthermore, I am convinced that even as ancient warriors at times needed help getting their belt (sash) wound tightly enough, so we need other people speaking the truth into our lives. This is one of the revelations on which I have built my life. I have built this way because I know the following things about myself:

♦   I can be deceived.
♦   I am not always right.
♦   I can be stubborn.

I realize that it is not the things I see that will destroy my life, family, or ministry; it is the things I do not see. Therefore, I make every effort to hear God's voice through the counsel, confrontation, and correction of the men God has placed in my life.

Furthermore, I am convinced one of best places for a pastor to find this type of accountability and authority is through the ministry of an apostle or an apostolic team. In some cases, the leader God brings the pastor into relationship with will be an apostle. In other cases, in the words of Peter Wagner, they will be hyphenated apostles such as an apostolic prophet, teacher, pastor, or evangelist. Whichever the case may be, they need to be leaders whose lives demonstrate a grace from God to plant and/or care for churches and the pastors who lead them. Men such as Michael Fletcher of Grace Churches International, Peter Beck of Master Builders, Emanuele Cannistraci of Apostolic Ministries International, and their apostolic teams on which they serve exemplify the grace I am describing.

Reason 3:   The power of apostolic association.

The third reason I believe an apostolic team is so important in the life of a senior pastor is what I will refer to as the power of apostolic and prophetic associations. Before I describe this power in the lives of senior pastors, however, let me talk about its affects in my own life. I am a better man and a better minister because of the apostles and prophets with whom I have been associated in friendship and teamwork over the years. I have never ceased to be both challenged by their visions and changed through their lives and messages. The apostles with whom I walk never allow me to become to complacent or too comfortable. There is always another church to plant or a nation to reach! When I become too myopic or too introspective, their passion to reach the whole world calls me back to the reality of why God put me on this planet in the first place. As for the prophets with whom I walk, time after time they have brought words of insight, direction, and protection into my life, the life of my family, and my ministry.

As for pastors, the benefits of walking with an apostle or a prophet are almost impossible to calculate. Whether it was an apostolic challenge to raise up more leaders or a prophecy about the growth God wanted to bring in the church they led, I have seen the lives of countless pastors changed through divine interaction with an apostolic team.

One of the finest examples of the power of apostolic association can be seen in the life of Phil Bonasso. One of the senior apostles in Morning Star International, Phil has been uniquely gifted by God to raise up leaders. A few years ago, one of our finest young campus pastors had been struggling for a year to plant a successful campus ministry on a hardened university. After days of praying for him, Phil met with him and challenged him to come into his divine destiny. In the years that followed, three or four hundred students were saved, the meeting grew to 200 in attendance, and numbers of the students were called into the ministry. What happened? In the words of that young man, it was a life-changing moment. He received an apostolic impartation which unlocked the faith and gifting he needed to be successful. This is only one example of the many I could site of the power of apostolic association.

Reason 4: Divine assignments.

The fourth reason for the ministry of an apostle or an apostolic team in the life of a pastor is divine assignments. Although prophets are involved in this process through the operation of the gifts of prophecy and the word of knowledge, this function is at the very essence of an apostle's ministry. As I stated in the first chapter, we must never forget that apostles are not just sent ones; they are senders. They have been commissioned by God to act as His divine sending agency. For example, in my own life, even though hearing God and being led by the Spirit are the very essence of my prophetic calling, I have been apostolically sent to places and people my prophetic gift alone would have never taken me. From professional sports franchises to college campuses, my life has been enriched through these apostolic assignments.

The experience of many senior pastors I know has been no different. As they have found and been fitted into the apostolic family where God has called them, they have found unique open doors and received incredible divine assignments. For example, in the Morning Star family of churches, we have a number of senior pastors doing the work of apostles in churches throughout the world. From pastoring other pastors to cooperating in church planting efforts, God has opened a larger world to them though the ministries of the apostles and prophets with whom they walk.

Reason 5: A Strategic Alliance

The fifth reason I consider apostolic relationships to be important in the lives of pastors is probably the most crucial of all. I say this because I believe the relationship between senior pastors and the apostolic team is absolutely vital to the fulfillment of God's plan to change this planet through the advance of His kingdom. Indeed this strategic alliance is the key to unlocking the resources needed to fulfill the Great Commission. In Ephesians 4:16, Paul himself comments on the strategic value of relationships in the body of Christ:

From whom the whole body, being fitted and held together by that which every joint supplies, according to the proper working of each individual part, causes the growth of the body for the building of itself in love (NAS).

What is Paul saying in this passage? The answer is simple, yet profound. Through healthy (properly working) relationships (joints), the body of Christ is supplied with what it needs to grow.

Let's take a moment now and apply this principle to the relationship between senior pastors and apostles. I say apostles because they, more than prophets or any other member of the apostolic team, have the critical role in this process. As for pastors, their role is vital because they are both the shepherds and the watchmen of their flocks. According to John 10:3, the watchmen determine who has access to the flock: *The watchman opens the gate for him, and the sheep listen to his voice. He calls his own sheep by name and leads them out.*

This access is important because the flock contains the resources needed to fulfill the Great Commission. As the watchman of the flock, the senior pastor has the awesome responsibility of determining how much access apostles will have to the manpower, money, and materials the congregation can provide. Therefore, the question of the hour for pastors is this: Will they allow their congregations to hear the voice of the apostolic?

The voice (ministry) of the apostle is essential, because through their gifting, the strategic potential of God's people is unlocked. When people are touched by the apostolic anointing, the effects can be amazing. Individuals who refused to work in the nursery now want to serve on a church planting team. People, who rarely gave more than a pittance, write checks for thousands. Like divine dynamite, the visionary gifting of the apostles has the ability to release fresh torrents of passion and service in the local church as the dams of lethargy and self-absorption are shattered.

If this essential joint, the relationship between apostles and senior pastors, is ever to supply what the body of Christ needs, two things are needed:

1. Apostles must be sensitive. By sensitive, I mean apostles must respect the place of the pastor in the church. This respect is critical because for years, pastors around the world have felt repeatedly robbed by predatory ministries who leave them out of the process while they sap finances and take the finest people, leaving them nothing in return.

In a healthy apostolic family, pastors are partners, not prey. They open their churches to the ministry of the apostles because they know their place and their role is honored and respected. They also know that money will never be solicited, nor their people recruited, without the their full partnership and blessing.

Furthermore, it is also essential the apostolic team place a high priority on the corporate needs of every church. Like the Apostle Paul, the apostles with whom God has called me to walk long to leave a life-giving deposit in every church they visit. Far from seeing the local churches and ministries that make up our family as a divine bank account to be drawn on until nothing is left, they burn to leave a deposit of apostolic faith, passion, and pattern everywhere they go. Although they desire to plant new churches, they are equally impassioned to see our existing churches reach their corporate destiny. Whether it is leadership training programs, or a ministry partnership arm which equips young campus workers to raise their own financial support, the apostles are doing everything they can to see each local church acquires the leadership base it needs in order to reach the harvest in their city.

2. Pastors must be strategic. Apostolic sensitivity alone is not enough to make the alliance work. Pastors must be willing to rise above the continual needs of their own church and ministry, to a place of apostolic purpose and passion. As they see the world strategically, they will be willing to release their finest leaders—and the money it takes to support them—in order to plant churches throughout their country and the world. They will also learn the same principles that apply to finances also apply to the training and release of leaders:

Remember this: Whoever sows sparingly will also reap sparingly, and whoever sows generously will also reap generously (2 Cor. 9:6). When a pastor is willing to generously sow leaders and finances into the larger world, that pastor will reap a harvest of new leaders and fresh financial provision that is beyond comprehension.

This type of partnership between senior pastors and apostolic teams, however, will take an incredible level of trust on the part of the senior pastor. First, the pastor must trust the Lord of the harvest to release the power, provision, and people needed to fulfill the church's local vision. Second, the senior pastor must trust the apostolic team with the people and provision God has placed under their stewardship. When God finds senior pastors and apostolic teams who are willing to walk in the levels of sensitivity, strategic thinking, and trust that type of partnership entails, the kingdom of hell will be shaken, and the kingdom of heaven will advance!

Barriers to Healthy
Apostle/Pastor Relationships

Sadly, for many pastors, trust is not a simple issue. Despite
the incredible benefits that come from senior pastors relating
to an apostle or an apostolic team, many of them never experience the reality of this relationship because they are unwilling
to deal with the barriers and impediments intrinsic to this process. For some pastors, the major barrier they face will be the
pain and disappointment of their own memories. Whether
they have felt abused by spiritual authority, or suffered the
trauma of a ministry that was destroyed through immorality,
financial impropriety, or authoritarianism, their innate distrust
of spiritual authority (and any form of organization larger than
the local church) is often greater than their need for its benefits.

Despite the reality of their pain, they face a critical choice.
Will they build on their wounds; or will they build on the
Word? In my own experience, I have found that the only
people who have never been wounded or disappointed by
authority are those who have never been under it. Therefore,
if we are to experience everything that God has for us, we
must be willing to go beyond our pain.

Barrier 1: Resistance from local church leadership.
For other pastors, however, the real barriers that need to be
overcome are in the lives of those around them. Many times,
the greatest barrier to a pastor's relationship with an apostolic
team is the resistance coming from his own local church leadership team. The pastoral staff, local elders, and other key

leaders in the church can be the greatest critics of what the pastor is proposing to do. When this is the case, the issues normally revolve around two things – trust and territory.

I say trust, because like the senior pastors they are serving, many local church leaders have had their own problems and disappointments with spiritual authority. These problems are compounded by the fact that, unlike their pastor, they will not have the have the quality time it normally takes to develop a relationship with the apostolic team member most involved in their church. This is important because relationships are at the very foundation of developing trust.

Barrier 2: Spiritual territory and authority.

The second barrier involves spiritual territory and authority. Let me take a moment to explain what I mean by this. In the absence of a functional apostolic team, a church staff and/or eldership teams have assumed the powers of an apostolic team. They oversee the pastor, direct church planting and missions, ordain other elders, and even govern the affairs of other churches planted out of the church they are serving. Therefore, it can be very threatening when the church they have been leading begins the process of aligning itself with an apostolic team. Although most of the leaders I have seen in this situation desire the will of God for the churches they are leading, the old patterns of authority and territory and the security they think they are losing can cause many problems.

Keys to Overcoming the Barriers

Despite the complexity of these barriers, many times even the most resistant staff members can be brought into a healthy relationship with the apostolic team. One model for how a senior pastor should approach this challenge can be found in the ministry of John the Baptist. Called to prepare the way for Jesus Christ, the great apostle (Heb. 3:1), he diligently worked to bond his followers with a man they hardly knew. There were several keys as to how he went about this:

Key 1: Preach apostolic importance.
In John's preaching, he clearly delineated the important place this apostolic figure held in the plan of God for their lives. Over and over again he announced the critical role that Jesus had been given:

The next day John saw Jesus coming toward him and said, "Look, the Lamb of God, who takes away the sin of the world! This is the one I meant when I said, 'A man who comes after me has surpassed me because he was before me.' I myself did not know him, but the reason I came baptizing with water was that he might be revealed to Israel" (John 1:29-31).

"I baptize you with water for repentance. But after me will come one who is more powerful than I, whose sandals I am not fit to carry. He will baptize you with the Holy Spirit and with fire. His winnowing fork is in his hand, and he will clear his threshing floor, gathering his wheat into the barn and burning up the chaff with unquenchable fire" (Matt. 3:11-12).

Key 2: Leaders' meetings.
John encouraged the leaders closest to him to accept the position Jesus had been given in their lives. This was more than theoretical; John's disciples went and spent the day with Jesus:
The next day John was there again with two of his disciples. When he saw Jesus passing by, he said, "Look, the Lamb of God!" When the two disciples heard him say this, they followed Jesus. Turning around, Jesus saw them following and asked, "What do you want?" They said, "Rabbi" (which means

Teacher), "where are you staying?"

"Come," he replied, "and you will see." So they went and saw where he was staying, and spent that day with him (John 1:35-39).

This is a significant point. It is not enough for the senior pastor to spend time with members of the apostolic team when they visit. A leaders' meeting should be a part of every apostolic visit. This gives the leaders of the local church both the opportunity to experience the anointing of the various team members as well as the occasion to interact with them. Times of fellowship around a meal are also great opportunities for the senior members of a local church's leadership team to get to know the members of the apostolic team. In these more intimate settings, deeper bonding can take place. Whatever we do, we must not waste these God-given moments.

Even if they never verbalize it, all leaders eventually ask the same question that John's leaders asked of Jesus: "Where are you staying?" Simply stated, they want to know the people to which the senior pastor has entrusted the church they are serving. That's why it is so important that both the senior pastor and the apostolic team members give the church leaders this opportunity.

If you are currently serving as a member of an apostolic team, this principle is also vital for you. Will you like Jesus, who Himself was already in the beginning of a nationwide ministry, say, "Come and see." When you are already tired from ministering, will you spend the time necessary to build a bond with the leaders of the local churches you are serving? How you answer this question may well define your relationship with the churches you have been called to watch over and protect.

Key 3: Understand God-given roles.

John refused to become insecure and defensive when the people in the ministry God had given him responded to the God-given role Jesus had in their life:

They came to John and said to him, "Rabbi, that man who was with you on the other side of the Jordan—the one you testified about—well, he is baptizing, and everyone is going to him." To this John replied, "A man can receive only what is given him from heaven" (John 3:26-27).

Many pastors can preach great messages on the place of apostles and prophets in the local church. However, their own insecurities limit their ability to make the lives of their people accessible to the ministries of other men.

Key 4: Regular times of fellowship.

The fourth key to dealing with barriers (involved in relationships between an apostolic team and local church leaders) is found in Deuteronomy 16:16:

Three times a year all your men must appear before the LORD your God at the place he will choose: at the Feast of Unleavened Bread, the Feast of Weeks and the Feast of Tabernacles. No man should appear before the LORD empty-handed.

Three times a year God required every male in Israel to come together to celebrate His blessing and provision on their nation. Why not two times or seven times? Although I am certainly not a sociologist, I believe a large group of people who are separated geographically must come together at least three times a year in order to maintain and perpetuate a spirit of faith and family.

In North America, the pastors in my spiritual family have committed to attending three of our conferences every year. They fellowship more often on a regional basis. Every local church staff member and elder is encouraged to attend our yearly national conference and the regional conference in their area.

These gatherings do not consist of just preaching and worship. There are times of fellowship, trips to amusement parks, banquets with entertainment, and golf tournaments.

Every leader is also encouraged to bring their whole family. This enables the local church leadership teams and their families to bond with their larger spiritual family as well as to receive vision and ministry from the members of the apostolic team. We are convinced: if we do not come together, we will not stay together. In this atmosphere, the bonds necessary for a lifetime of ministry and relationship can be formed. Even if the elders can only make it to one or two of these gatherings, they can still receive the revelation and the impartation they need to confidently embrace the vision of their larger apostolic family.

To Summarize...

Let's take a moment now, to summarize the major points of this chapter:

1. Senior pastors need accountability for their lives, families, and ministries.

2. Senior pastors and their churches need the covering and authority provided by apostolic government, for without authority no real accountability or spiritual protection is possible.

3. One of the best places for accountability and spiritual authority to be found is through an apostle or

another member of an apostolic team.

4.   Senior pastors will grow as people and ministers through their association with an apostolic team.

5.   Senior pastors can step into the next level of their calling and gifting through the opportunities provided by assignments coming through the ministry of apostles and prophets.

6.   The relationship between senior pastors and apostles is especially crucial to the advance of God's Kingdom.

7.   Whether they have felt abused by spiritual author- ity or suffered the trauma of a ministry that was destroyed through immorality, financial impropriety, or authoritarianism, some pastors will have to deal with the barriers of their own pain and disappoint- ments before they can relate to an apostolic team.

8.   In some cases, the greatest barrier to a senior pastor's relationship with an apostolic team will be the attitudes, insecurities, and perceptions of the pas- toral staff and the local elders.

9.   Like John the Baptist, who prepared his disciples for the ministry of Jesus, senior pastors must preach on the role of the apostolic team and provide oppor- tunities for their leaders to be under the ministry of the team's members.

I am convinced that when God finds senior pastors and apostolic teams who are willing to walk in the levels of sensitivity, strategic thinking, and trust, we will experience new levels of church planting and Kingdom advancement. This advancement, however, will also bring new levels of warfare. We must never forget just the potential of these relationships is enough to bring the diabolical assaults of hell. Whether you are an apostolic team member, a pastor, or the member of a local church leadership team, you must vigilantly guard this relationship from the satanic accusations and subterfuge that is sure to come. You must guard it, because the relationship between the apostolic team and the senior pastor is the strategic essence of God's plan to transform the cities and nations of our world.

CHAPTER SIX

MAINTAINING APOSTOLIC PARTNERSHIPS

T hroughout this book, I have attempted to answer one simple question: "Can apostles, prophets, senior pastors, and local church leaders work together as a team to change the world?" Let us never forget that if it were easy, everyone would do it. A highly successful megachurch pastor once made the following statement: "If history has proven anything, it has proven that strong apostolic leaders cannot walk together." After his wife divorced him, a friend of mine restated his sentiments: "If history has proven anything, it has proven that strong apostolic leaders had better walk together." Yet, despite the power of these partnerships, by their very nature they are fraught with peril.

Lessons From a Divine Ministry Team

An example of the pressures that come to destroy these divine partnerships can be found in the story of history's most important ministry team. These partners were cousins. Both of them were birthed supernaturally: one came from a virgin, and the other came from the barren womb of an aging woman. Only months apart in age, they had grown up on the stories of the divine calling which surrounded their lives. Their names were Jesus and John the Baptist.

There can be no doubt that their partnership was divinely originated. John was an anointed prophet, sent to prepare the world for the ministry of his cousin, God's only Son.

In those days John the Baptist came, preaching in the Desert of Judea and saying, "Repent, for the kingdom of heaven is near." This is he who was spoken of through the prophet Isaiah: "A voice of one calling in the desert, 'Prepare the way for the Lord, make straight paths for him'" (Matt. 3:1-3).

Yet at the end of his life, John was assailed with doubts about the very partnership to which he had been called by God. Let's take a moment now to examine the principles and pressures of apostolic partnerships from the lives of Jesus and John.

Principle 1: Understand your self-perceptions.

Now this was John's testimony when the Jews of Jerusalem sent priests and Levites to ask him who he was. He did not fail to confess, but confessed freely, "I am not the Christ." They asked him, "Then who are you? Are you Elijah?" He said, "I am not." "Are you the Prophet?" He answered, "No" (John 1:19-21).

Like John, every leader must answer these questions. At times, out of the morass of our own insecurities, they will be whispered to us by the enemy. At other times, they will come in the form of a compliment from a well-meaning Christian.

However they come, our response reveals our self-perception. These self-perceptions (how we see ourselves) can determine both the depth and the shape of our divine partnerships.

The first question is critical. "Are you the Christ (Messiah)?" Of course we are not Jesus Christ; anyone knows that! No, the question is far more subtle than that: "Do we have a Messianic complex?" Do we believe (deep down) that we are God's hope, maybe even His singular hope, for our nation, city, or church? If this delusive complex begins to take root in our soul, we will lose all of our felt need to walk in partnership with other leaders.

Next: "Are you Elijah?" What is our model for ministry? In our own minds, are we the lone prophet on the hill –the last one standing? Do we see ourselves as the only leader who has really never bowed a knee to the Baals of our culture? If this is our perception, we may never meet the other seven thousand leaders who are also battling and standing around us (1 Kings 19:9-10;18).

Last: "Are you the prophet?" You know what I mean— "The man"—the one who has all the anointing, answers, and wisdom necessary for any situation. As long as we believe we are "the man," we will never truly be part of anything larger than our own gifts can produce.

Principle 2: **Cultivate consistency, honesty, and humility.**
The next principle is found in John's answer to these vital questions. *"He did not fail to confess, but confessed freely"* (John 1:20) he was not the Messiah, not Elijah, and not the prophet. He not only gave the right answers, he gave them consistently and honestly. By consistently, I mean his answers were always the same. Unlike some leaders, who give one confession to their peers but display a whole different attitude around their staff and congregation, John consistently

resisted the temptation of ego and pride.

Furthermore, John's answers were not motivated by the pressures of religious protocol or the desire to appear humble in the eyes of other leaders. The definitive answer he finally gave the religious leaders of his day gives us an incredible window into John's heart:

John replied in the words of Isaiah the prophet, "I am the voice of one calling in the desert, 'Make straight the way for the Lord.'" Now some Pharisees who had been sent questioned him, "Why then do you baptize if you are not the Christ, nor Elijah, nor the Prophet?"

"I baptize with water," John replied, "but among you stands one you do not know. He is the one who comes after me, the thongs of whose sandals I am not worthy to untie" (John 1:23-27).

What was John saying? "I'm only part of a team; I am just the voice of One who is far more anointed than I will ever be." John understood what some never understand. Until we realize that our ministry or anointing is not the whole story, we will never be willing to simply play our part. Sadly, without the willingness to simply be a part, we will never experience the true joy and fulfillment of partnership.

Principle 3: See others as God sees them.

"I would not have known him, except that the one who sent me to baptize with water told me, 'The man on whom you see the Spirit come down and remain is he who will baptize with the Holy Spirit.' I have seen and I testify that this is the Son of God" (John 1:33-34).

At first, this passage doesn't seem to make sense. John had known Jesus all of his life. Surely he had the stories of his father's prophecy and his mother's divine encounter with Mary, mother of Jesus? Yet, he said he did not really know his cousin until he saw heaven's dove land on Him. Could it be that the Father realized that family ties, a shared heritage, and joint destiny were not enough to maintain John's understanding of who his cousin really was? Was this what the Apostle Paul meant when he said it is was not enough *"to regard people from a worldly point of view "* (2 Cor. 5:16)?

In my own experience, I have found things such as a common history, the same vision, and natural affinities are not enough to keep strong, anointed leaders working together. We must see the dove in the lives of those with whom we work. In fact, is not enough to simply see the dove land. Even when we are challenged by the quirks of their personality or offended by something they did or said, we must not lose sight of the fact that the dove of calling and anointing still remains. Are we spiritual enough to see our "partners" as the Holy Spirit sees them? This question is at the very essence of maintaining divine partnerships.

Principle 4: **Relate to and receive from other team members.**

John built into his disciples the ability to relate to and receive from other members of the ministry team (John 1:35-39):

The next day John was there again with two of his disciples. When he saw Jesus passing by, he said, "Look, the Lamb of God!" When the two disciples heard him say this, they followed Jesus. Turning around, Jesus saw them following and asked, "What do you want?" They said, "Rabbi" (which means Teacher), "where are you staying?" "Come," he replied, "and you will see." So they went and saw where he was staying, and spent that day with him. It was about the tenth hour.

In our spiritual family, we have found that whether you

are a part of the apostolic team or a local church leadership team, this principle is critical for at least three reasons:

First, even though John and Jesus had the maturity to walk together, their competitive young disciples created tensions between them (John 3:22-26):

After this, Jesus and his disciples went out into the Judean countryside, where he spent some time with them, and baptized. Now John also was baptizing at Aenon near Salim, because there was plenty of water, and people were constantly coming to be baptized. (This was before John was put in prison.) An argument developed between some of John's disciples and a certain Jew over the matter of ceremonial washing. They came to John and said to him, "Rabbi, that man who was with you on the other side of the Jordan—the one you testified about—well, he is baptizing, and everyone is going to him."

Whether it is the problem described here—or the immature competitiveness Paul describes between his disciples and the disciples of Peter and Apollos (1 Cor. 1:10-12)—this is still an issue today. Young disciples tend to perceive their immediate spiritual family just as natural children perceive their blood family: "It is the best!" No other father or family even comes close. Although part of this is only a stage all natural and spiritual children go through, we must build into the people we disciple a deep appreciation and respect for *every* leader in our spiritual family.

Second, like John, we must walk in the revelation that one person's gifting is not normally enough to bring a person or a people into everything God has for them. Even as Jesus the apostle was needed to finish the work John had started in his disciple Andrew, so the leaders I am discipling need the ministry of other gifted leaders.

The importance of building the lives of people through a

team can also be seen in Paul's answer to the spiritual competition rampant in the church of Corinth:

What, after all, is Apollos? And what is Paul? Only servants, through whom you came to believe—as the Lord has assigned to each his task. I planted the seed, Apollos watered it, but God made it grow. So neither he who plants nor he who waters is anything, but only God, who makes things grow. The man who plants and the man who waters have one purpose, and each will be rewarded according to his own labor. For we are God's fellow workers; you are God's field, God's building (1 Cor. 3:5-9).

Paul realized that he, Peter, and Apollos all had a part to play in the divine purpose of helping the believers in the church at Corinth to grow. It is no different today. Great churches and strong disciples are built best through a team.

Third, when an individual is only anchored in a church or ministry through one relationship, it is very easy for him or her to be dislodged. Let me explain what I mean by this: Sooner or later, misunderstanding and the temptation to become offended comes to test every relationship. When a person has learned to receive from more than one member of the leadership team, however, he or she will have a another mature person to turn to when the moment of relational testing comes.

Principle 5: **Live for a common vision.**

The fifth principle of maintaining team ministry is found in the response of John and Jesus to the competitive spirit tearing at the very fabric of their relationship:

To this John replied, "A man can receive only what is given him from heaven. You yourselves can testify that I said, 'I am not the Christ but am sent ahead of him.' The bride belongs to the bridegroom. The friend who attends the bride-

groom waits and listens for him, and is full of joy when he hears the bridegroom's voice. That joy is mine, and it is now complete (John 3:27-29).

The Pharisees heard that Jesus was gaining and baptizing more disciples than John, although in fact it was not Jesus who baptized, but his disciples. When the Lord learned of this, he left Judea and went back once more to Galilee (John 4:1-3).

As we can see from the above passages, John was seemingly losing his ministry to Jesus. This was important because more than attendance figures and television ratings were at stake. The crowds were keeping Herod from arresting Jesus. Yet, when faced with the loss of his ministry and the possible loss of his life, John answer was incredible: "I can only play the part given to me from heaven." My joy is not based on the response of people to my ministry; it is based on people finding the bridegroom (the Messiah). It is no different in our lives today. When we, like John, live to build God's Kingdom instead of our own little kingdoms, there will be no place for competition and jealousy.

What about the response of Jesus to this situation? When He perceived that His rising fame and stature were adversely affecting the ministry of John, He left the heart of the nation and returned to the provincial obscurity of Galilee. The reason for this was simple. He was more interested in the success and safety of John's life and ministry than He was in His own success.

The responses of Jesus and John provide a critical model for our hour. Are we willing to live for a common vision, even if it means our role decreases and our part is obscured? Can we place the success of another leader over our own? These are the questions that will determine the quality of the team ministry we experience in the years to come.

Principle 6: **Allow differences to create a divine symphony.**

The next two principles of team ministry from the lives of Jesus and John are found in Matthew 11:1-3:

After Jesus had finished instructing his twelve disciples, he went on from there to teach and preach in the towns of Galilee. When John heard in prison what Christ was doing, he sent his disciples to ask him, "Are you the one who was to come, or should we expect someone else?"

What a tragic turn their relationship had taken! John—the very man called to reveal Jesus to the world—was now doubting Him. Surely blood ties, shared destiny, natural affinity, and abundant supernatural signs would have been foundation enough for their relationship to be maintained. Obviously, they weren't enough of a foundation. What had happened?

The answer to this question is found in the passage, *"...when John heard in prison what Christ was doing."* From this passage, we find that John was doubting both the reality of who Jesus was and the validity of their own relationship. His doubt stemmed from what he had heard and where he was when he heard it.

Let's start with what John heard. Although we do not know the exact words, it is clear from the following passage that Jesus and John had very different ministry styles:

For John came neither eating nor drinking, and they say, "He has a demon." The Son of Man came eating and drinking, and they say, "Here is a glutton and a drunkard, a friend of tax collectors and sinners." But wisdom is proved right by her actions (Matt 11:18-19).

John, the austere prophet, preached a strong message of repentance and lived in the desert—totally separated from the world. On the other hand, Jesus the great Apostle and Evangelist turned water into wine, frequented parties, and fellowshipped with people of questionable character. To John, this must have bordered on serious spiritual compromise. In fact, in John 3:25, we find that some of John's disciples even argued with Jesus about His concept of holiness. Tragically, the very differences offending John (Matt. 11:6) were also the very reasons God had called them together.

To explain, John was a divine plow called to breakup the hardened top soil of religious Judaism. To that end, he was rigid, uncompromising and austere. Jesus, on the other hand, was destined to plant the church in the soil John had broken up. Although He was unflinching in His defense of the truth, His manner was open, loving, and approachable, except when He was dealing with the hypocrisy of the religious leaders.

It is no different with the team of leaders on which I serve. Many of us are very different in personality, approach, and even giftings. Although we are all either apostles or prophets, our secondary giftings can vary radically. These differences, under the control of the Holy Spirit, can create a divine symphony as every member finds and fulfills their God-given role. Yet without the maturity and security necessary to walk through and even enjoy the tensions created by our differences, we would be rife with discord and division.

Principle 7: **Be prepared for relationships to be tested.**

When John heard in prison what Christ was doing, he sent his disciples (Matt. 11:2).

As I said earlier, John's doubt was based both on what he had heard about Jesus and where he was when he heard it. Where was John? John was in prison. That's right, no longer protected by the size of his ministry, John had been cast into prison for condemning Herod's illicit marriage. Now as he sat isolated in the clammy darkness of his cell, he begin to question both the reason for his existence and the primary relationship to which he had been called. Imagine the thoughts beginning to rise in his mind:

"If He was really who He said He was, He'd do one of those miracles I have been hearing about and set me free."

"He stole all my disciples; maybe He has everything He wants now."

"If His message wasn't filled with compromise, He'd be in this prison with me now."

"That pretender has abandoned me."

Sadly, John was no different than you and me. Whether it is demonic or purely circumstantial, when we feel imprisoned emotionally, physically, financially, or spiritually, our sense of reality gradually becomes distorted. In that state, we can easily question our most cherished relationships and foundational values. Like John, as our sense of isolation grows, we even send messages through third parties to the people from whom we feel estranged.

When this test comes (and it will), we must do three things: First, we have to call to mind the fact that God has divinely placed us into the very relationships now under assault. Second, when there is a real offense involved, we must communicate with the person who has offended us and deal with the offense biblically. Third, it is critical we resist every lie and distorted perception the enemy brings to our mind.

Knots in God's Divine Net

In closing, right principles alone will not protect the apostolic partnerships in which God has called us to walk. Whether you are an apostle, prophet, senior pastor, or a local church leader, sooner or later the enemy will assault the primary relationships in your life. At that moment, natural affinity, joint history, and common vision may not be enough to stem the tide of pain and misunderstanding which has grown from a trickle to a rushing torrent in your soul.

Whether it is a simple misunderstanding, a complex offense, or a clouded misperception, we must fight for the relationships to which God has called us. We must fight because these relationships are not just about our spiritual health. They are about the harvest! In Matthew 13:47, we find that God forms the lives of His people into a net for the harvest:

Once again, the kingdom of heaven is like a net that was let down into the lake and caught all kinds of fish.

I am convinced the divine relationships and partnerships God calls us into are the knots of this net. Church history is fraught with stories of division and schism because the relationships of the people God used were not strong enough to bear the tests and trials that always come. In this hour, may God weave our lives together into the fiber of apostolic partnerships strong enough to bear the weight of heaven's harvest and the fury of hell's assault.

SUBJECT INDEX

Seven Power Principles

That I Didn't Learn in Seminary

C. Peter Wagner

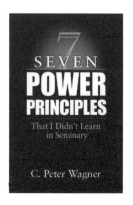

God is moving with power in the world today! In this book, Wagner captures 7 key principles for moving in that power.

"God is alive and active today but the evidence of His activity is often difficult to find in Evangelical seminaries and the churches pastored by seminary graduates. Peter Wagner is a standard-bearer for the growing numbers of Christian leaders and churches that are moving with God beyond the drag of intellectualism. This book is a worthy summary of what God has been teaching many of us since seminary. I pray that God will use it to point the way for many more church leaders to follow the Holy Spirit's guidance beyond what they learned in seminary."

Dr. Charles Kraft
Professor of Anthropology and Intercultural Communication
Fuller Theological Seminary, Pasadena, California

Leadership/Spiritual Warfare
Paperback • 86p
ISBN 1-58502-014-1 • $7.00

Available at finer bookstores
or by calling toll-free 888-563-5150

Apostles of the City

How to Mobilize Territorial Apostles for City Transformation

C. Peter Wagner

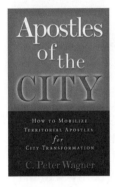

In recent years the Body of Christ has seen some important principles for city transformation set in place. While there have been many short-term successes, city after city reports that their efforts over the long haul are not producing the city transformation that they have worked so hard to accomplish.

So, what are we missing? How can we see our cities become all that God intended them to be? This book examines how recognizing and affirming apostles of the city might well be the most vital missing link for seeing our cities truly transformed!

Discover the answers to many questions, including:

- What strategic changes need to be made in my city in order to see it truly transformed?

- Who is an "apostle of the city," and how are they set in place?

- What are the three crucial concepts I need to know that will lay the proper groundwork for city transformation?

- Is my city prepared for the moving of the Holy Spirit that will bring real transformation in the near future?

This important new book is for everyone who wants to see their city move beyond short-term successes into the genuine transformation that God desires to bring!

Leadership
Paperback • 58p
ISBN 1.58502.006.0 • $6.00

Pastors & Prophets
Protocol for Healthy Churches

C. Peter Wagner, Editor

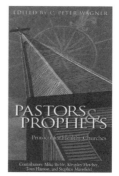

Pastors need prophets! Their churches will be healthier with them than without them. Prophets often help take the local church to another level of experiencing God's power that pastors long for. So why, then, do pastors and prophets often have a difficult time relating to each other as the Lord intended?

In this book, C. Peter Wagner has assembled four widely respected, hands-on pastors who have proven track records of establishing positive and productive relationships with prophets. Together they answer many vital questions including:

- Why are pastors intimidated by prophets?

- Why are prophets often hurt by pastors?

- How can pastors help prophets mature in their gift?

- Who is the pastor-prophet relationship is the ultimate authority?

- What protocol can pastors and prophets follow that will cause their churches to be healthy and well equipped?

As pastors and prophets come into a proper relationship with each other, they have a unique opportunity to propel the church forward with power and vision. This book is an essential tool toward making the pastor-prophet relationship all it can be!

Contributors: Mike Bickle, Kingsley Fletcher, Tom Hamon, and Stephen Mansfield.

Leadership
Paperback • 81p
ISBN 1.58502.015.X • $7.00

Revival!

It Can Transform Your City

C. Peter Wagner

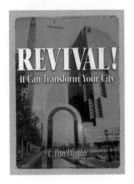

This book takes you beyond city taking to city transformation!

Questions addressed include:

- What exactly is revival?

- Can a city actually be transformed through revival?

- How can Christians move to new levels of spiritual warfare to see revival come?

- What new wineskins is the Holy Spirit using to facilitate revival?

- What steps can be taken to sustain revival in a city?

Discover how the Spirit of God can visibly transform cities through the revival we have been praying for.

Leadership/Spiritual Warfare
Paperback • 63p
ISBN 0.9667481.8.2 • $6.00

Radical Holiness For Radical Living

C. Peter Wagner

Holiness has long been a topic of great debate. In this easy-to-read book, C. Peter Wagner helps bring clarity to the topic by answering many questions including:

- Can anyone really live a holy life?

- Is there a test of holiness?

- What are the non-negotiable principles for radical holiness?

- How much holiness should be required of a leader?

For any believer who wants to be everything God wants them to be, this book will open the way for them to move to new levels in their Christian lives. Through radical holiness, readers will learn to defeat Satan's schemes and enjoy daily victory in their walk with God!

Christian Living
Paperback • 41p
ISBN 0.9667481.1.5 • $6.00

Available at finer bookstores
or by calling toll-free 888-563-5150

The Breaker Anointing

God's Power to Press Through

Barbara J. Yoder

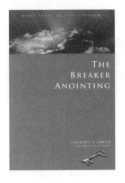

It's time to break forth! God is empowering a new breed of believers to break open territories and press through into greater levels of victory and power than ever before. In this revolutionary book, Pastor Barbara Yoder introduces Jesus as the "Breaker." It is His breaker anointing that will enable you to pass through the gate in order to see breakthrough come into your life, your church, and your city.

"The truths found within this book will give you the wisdom and faith you need to obtain the greatest breakthrough of your life. This book also shows you how to receive the breaker anointing and will help you minister breakthrough to others as well."
Dr. Bill Hamon, President/Founder
Christian International Ministries Network

Christian Living
Paperback • 89p
ISBN 1-58502-017-6• $7.00

Ridding Your Home
of Spiritual Darkness

Chuck D. Pierce
& Rebecca Wagner Sytsema

Christians are often completely unaware of how
the enemy has gained access to their homes
through what they own. This practical, easy-to-
read book can be used by any Christian to pray
through their home and property in order to
close the door to the enemy and experience
richer spiritual life. Included are chapters on
children, sin, generational curses, and spiritual

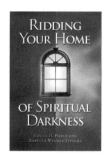

discernment, as well as a step-by-step guide to praying through
your home and a section of questions and answers.

Christian Living Paperback • 80p
ISBN 1-58502-008-7 • $7.00

Receiving the Word
of the Lord

Chuck D. Pierce
& Rebecca Wagner Sytsema

The Bible makes it very clear that God has a
plan for our lives. By hearing and receiving the
voice of God, we can know our purpose and
destiny. In this book you will discover how to
hear the voice of God, develop an understanding of prophecy, learn how to test a prophetic
word, and experience the joy of responding to
God's voice.

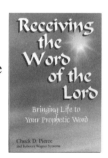

Christian Living Paperback • 43p
ISBN 0-9667481-2-3 • $6.00

Available at finer bookstores
or by calling toll-free 888-563-5150